William T. Tappan, Jr., an experienced Realtor* specializing in commercial and investment real estate, is the past Director of the Albuquerque Board of Realtors.

The Real Estate Acquisition Handbook

Money-Making Techniques For The Serious Investor

William T. Tappan

A SPECTRUM BOOK

PRENTICE-HALL, INC. Englewood Cliffs, N.J. 07632

Library of Congress Cataloging in Publication Data

Tappan, William T 1943–
The real estate acquisition handbook.

(A Spectrum book)
Includes index.
1. Real estate investment. I. Title.
HD1375.T36 332.6'324 79-20347
ISBN 0-13-762633-9
ISBN 0-13-762625-8 pbk.

For Dad, DuBie, and Edith

Editorial/production supervision by Donald Chanfrau
Interior design by Jeannette Jacobs
Cover design by Tony Ferrara
Manufacturing buyers: Cathie Lenard and Barbara Frick

A SPECTRUM BOOK

10 9 8 7 6 5 4 3 2

Printed in the United States of America

PRENTICE-HALL INTERNATIONAL, INC., *London*
PRENTICE-HALL OF AUSTRALIA PTY. LIMITED, *Sydney*
PRENTICE-HALL OF CANADA, LTD., *Toronto*
PRENTICE-HALL OF INDIA PRIVATE LIMITED, *New Delhi*
PRENTICE-HALL OF JAPAN, INC., *Tokyo*
PRENTICE-HALL OF SOUTHEAST ASIA PTE. LTD., *Singapore*
WHITEHALL BOOKS LIMITED, WELLINGTON, *New Zealand*

Contents

Foreword

As one who writes about and teaches real estate finance, I know that it is an extremely difficult subject. So whenever I see mention of a book or article on the topic, I immediately send away for a copy. And I am usually disappointed.

Bill Tappan's *The Real Estate Acquisition Handbook* is a notable exception. Bill seems to possess the ideal combination of intelligence, experience, education, and determination for the real estate investing field. Where other authors tend to get too theoretical, too simplistic, or too technical, Bill offers thoughtful creativity tempered by a recognition of the practical problems of making acquisitions in the real world.

Many real estate authors seize upon a particular boom period and proclaim that real estate investing can't miss. Bill Tappan has been around long enough, and remembers well enough, to know that this isn't so. He presents a sober, realistic description of both the rewards *and* risks in real estate investing and financing and tells the reader how to negotiate the dangerous waters safely.

Acquisition techniques often have income tax ramifications. Fortunately for the reader, Bill has a strong tax background and points out the pertinent tax implications as he proceeds.

One can picture a buyer and seller who want to make a deal, but can't figure out how, thumbing through *The Real Estate Acquisition Handbook* at the negotiating table. If there's a way to do it, Bill Tappan has probably described it in these pages. This is a realistic, practical, understandable compendium of real estate acquisition techniques, a welcome guide to the, as yet, relatively uncharted waters of real estate finance. I believe the knowledge it offers will enable its readers to make deals they would not otherwise have tried and to salvage deals that otherwise would have been lost. And I expect *The Real Estate Acquisition Handbook* to become a necessary reference for those who acquire real estate, and for those Realtors and attorneys who facilitate the acquisition of real estate.

John T. Reed
Real estate investor and author
San Francisco

Preface

This book is designed to help you acquire real estate. It is composed of specific techniques that cut through problems to help you meet your real estate acquisition objectives.

A cash purchase is only one of the hundreds of ways to acquire real estate. Many of the most effective methods rely entirely on terms worked out with property owners who don't even want an immediate large cash payment.

It is this flexibility that adds to the natural advantage inherent in real estate. Chapter 1 covers the characteristics of real estate that set it apart from other types of investments and give it the edge for people who are serious about becoming financially secure.

Our economy is growing increasingly volatile. Chapter 2 gives you a perspective and framework for judging the timing and location of your real estate activity.

Real estate analysis, to a large degree, is learning how to use your own good judgment. Chapter 3 covers the easy-to-use methods you can apply to any investment to decide the level of risk and profit.

If you're starting out on your real estate acquisition program and don't have a lot of cash, you'll find Chapter 4 quite helpful. It contains thirty-two techniques for acquiring real estate when you don't have cash.

Investing in real estate is a process of negotiating and structuring financing. Scores of methods designed to set up real estate financing are covered in Chapters 5, 6, and 7.

Chapters 8 and 9 deal with useful applications of leases and options in real estate acquisition. Chapter 10 contains techniques that you can apply to increase value, solve problems, and protect yourself.

This is a book of practical techniques. These street-wise methods are the result of years of actual real estate practice by investors and brokers throughout the United States. They are the formulas that power the incredibly swift rise to financial independence of people from all walks of life, and now they can do the same for you.

William T. Tappan, Jr.

1

You Have A Natural Advantage With Real Estate

2

You Have A Natural Advantage With Real Estate

Real estate is one of the few investments that can provide financial security and independence as a result of your own initiative. You don't need a lot of money or a lot of specialized technical knowledge to get started. An average amount of common sense, consistent effort, and a desire to learn will put you far ahead fast.

This point was illustrated by John Gray who inquired about a group of commercial buildings I had advertised for sale. Although John didn't buy the property (a fact he often lamented later), he did reveal his interesting and very successful acquisition strategy.

John was a draftsman who spent his coffee breaks and lunch hours searching the local newspapers for new real estate ads. His objective was to read the paper *every* day and get to the good buys before the other guys. John was so successful that his supervisor at work couldn't stand it and looked for any excuse to cause him trouble at work. The supervisor envied John's life style. He had acquired a country estate, drove a sports car, owned land and income property, and actually made more money from his lunch hour searches than from his job.

Finally, the envy and mystery got to John's boss who found a minor excuse and fired him. This was all he needed to devote full time to real estate acquisition. John's lunch hour real estate projects actually forced job independence on him in less than three years. Consistent effort provided the experience, and with time real estate freed him from the necessity of working for others. Now he works by choice and with considerably greater compensation, acquiring and selling investment real estate.

FOUR REASONS WHY YOU HAVE AN ADVANTAGE WITH INCOME REAL ESTATE

It's the nature of real estate that gives you the edge. And in today's investment climate we need all the help we can get. Certain characteristics of real estate make it destined to play an increasingly important role in our lives over the years to come.

There's no sure-thing investment, and every opportunity involving money warrants caution. Nevertheless, each type of investment has somewhat of a personality that is reflected in its price behavior. You can actually learn about the market behavior of different types of investments by watching their price action. Ultimately, how much money an investment takes out or puts in your pocket is determined by its price fluctuation. For example, real estate tends to be more stable than the stock market. It has certain characteristics that work in your favor.

The objective of investment is to make money. Whether you want money for financial security or to spend on the good life, or both, is up to you. Regardless of your purpose, you may already realize that real estate acquisition is one of the most controllable and likely methods to meet your financial objectives. There are in fact four major advantages inherent in the ownership of income real estate.

1. Cash Flow. Rental income from improved real estate is one of the few sources of relatively passive income. Cash flow from income property is for the most part produced by the capital asset itself as distinguished from earnings that result from your personal efforts. Consequently, you can set up a situation that in effect provides you with a salary, but does not place the demands on your time that a job does. Furthermore, by being able to raise rents as inflation warrants you have an advantage over many jobs. Rental income results from ownership, not employment, and that's the basis of the security it offers for you.

2. Equity Build-up. Usually real estate acquisitions are structured with financing that covers the majority of the cost. As the loans are paid off (often with the rental income produced by the property), your equity builds up; that is, the portion of your ownership which is free and clear of debt increases. When you consider that the loan is paid off from tenants' rent, it's easy to visualize equity build-up as a savings account, increased each month by a kind benefactor and available for use when you sell.

3. Appreciation. Appreciation is another natural characteristic which works to increase your equity. Normal investment appreciation results from the interaction between supply and demand in the marketplace. This is true of real estate, but more consistently so. There is a *very* long history of gradual increase in the value of land—the basis of real estate. Of course, the speed of appreciation varies depending on the supply-demand balance in a given location at a given time. Appreciation of real property is sometimes distorted by overheated speculation and surprise deflation, but historically values have increased steadily with population growth as the supply of land decreases relative to demand.

4. Tax Shelter. Tax shelter usually refers to the *artificial* (not actual) loss that results from depreciation of improved real property. This is a double advantage. Often rents and salary income can be sheltered from income tax. It's this effect that has made real estate such a sought-after investment among high-income bracket investors. It works very simply. As improved real estate wears out, the law *requires* you to depreciate a certain percentage of the value of the improvements as an operating expense. It is deducted from rental income each year. If the depreciation exceeds the rental income when combined with other operating expenses, it is then deducted from your additional income, thereby "sheltering" it from tax.

This has become an increasingly popular benefit of real estate as inflation has forced so many people into higher percentage tax brackets, while higher living costs have eroded real purchasing power.

Cash flow, equity build-up, appreciation, and tax shelter are the measurable benefits normally associated with real estate. They each contribute to tangible profit when you eventually establish the total return on income-producing real estate. Each benefit has value that can be measured.

REAL ESTATE HAS THE EDGE

It's more likely that you will become rich if you own real estate. If you have made the decision to accumulate wealth (regardless of your personal reasons), your probability of success is greatly increased if real estate ownership is part of your plan. If you are already wealthy, the chances of keeping the real value of your estate are also increased when you own real estate.

If you don't have much to start with, it's a slow process to build an estate by trading stocks. This is true even if you're an expert—simply because of the nature of the stock market. Of course, the ownership of a well-timed purchase of stocks has a place in a balanced investment portfolio, but when you're first starting out the odds are in your favor with real estate.

Years ago, one young professional found he had about $1,200 left after a prolonged effort at beating the stock market. Because he had just married, he decided it was time to get serious and make some money. He closed his brokerage account, took the $1,200, and made a down payment on a rental house. Over the next four months he borrowed down payments for a triplex and duplex. Within one year he had regained all the money lost in the stock market. Soon he quit his job, started wheeling and dealing in real estate, and was financially independent five years later. As he told it: "I finally noticed that the people who made money and kept it did it by acquiring real estate."

You can verify the relative performance of people who apply concentrated effort in real estate and those who follow the financial markets. Just look at the people you know. How many are more secure in their real estate portfolio than in their stock market efforts? If you want to go a step farther to get a statistical reading on your chances, check the rate of success on bank trusts that invest in the financial markets (but shy away from real estate). It doesn't matter how much money you make from time to time if you can't hang on to it.

The point is that it takes a high degree of specialized skill to succeed in trading financial markets and usually several years of painful financial losses, not to mention a reasonably large nest egg to practice with. Financial markets have their place, but the wide, difficult-to-predict fluctuations place a heavy burden on even experienced money managers.

In contrast, real estate has certain unique characteristics that work in your favor. It is a forgiving investment. If you make a mistake you can apply a few techniques, adjust the financing, wait for the right time, and sell out to a more appropriate owner, usually at a reasonable profit.

One of the interesting aspects of real estate is that at certain times certain property just seems to be right for certain people. A friend of mine actually specializes in acquiring property in a ten-block stretch of one street. It's a run-down area that he knows like a book and he makes money hand over fist.

What may appear to be a disaster for one person is the foundation of prosperity for another. It's just this characteristic of real estate that can often form a hidden opportunity for your estate building program. Finding property that someone else doesn't want is the starting point. The more they don't want it, the better your chances of negotiating a favorable acquisition.

Another aspect of real estate that gives you an edge is its traditionally inseparable dependence on credit. You're really not expected to pay cash for real estate. In many cases you don't even need approved credit. Negotiated leverage is expected and is an indispensable advantage when you know the full range of financing techniques available. Normal down payments can range from virtually nothing on certain government-backed mortgages to 25% down on many bank-financed commercial projects. There are no absolutes in financing real estate.

It's your negotiation ability that often makes or breaks the deal. It's in your hands. Certainly, what you can do will vary with different lenders and different sellers. Just don't give up until you find the right ones.

There are no standard requirements for cash outlays in real estate. Many new projects are totally put together with loans. Developers actually try to "mortgage out" by limiting their costs to the amount of the construction financing. Sellers have even been known to give the buyer cash. In some privately financed transactions the purchaser is sometimes paid by the seller as an incentive to take property.

These, of course, are extreme examples, but they point out the vast range of opportunities available to anyone who knows even a small percentage of the several techniques which can be customized to acquire real estate.

YOU HAVE MORE CONTROL WITH REAL ESTATE

There is one characteristic of real estate ownership that can work in your favor or against you: control. From beginning to end, from acquisition to sale, you personally have the helm. It's your thought and action that must determine your decisions and the success of the acquisition. The techniques you use to negotiate low risk and maximum profit in the beginning, the problems of ownership and management, and the final sale decisions maybe years later, all rest on you. It's your thought and your action that control the outcome.

Owning investment real estate is not unlike owning a small business. It's just easier. If the real estate market turns against you, time and patience can often bring you out on top eventually. If a small business topples, normally you're just out of business (unless you're especially talented).

Real estate offers any number of problem-solving opportunities. You can divide the property, increase or lower the rents, upgrade the appearance, restructure the financing, and take any number of steps to make a personal effort that will protect your investment.

Really, this type of concentrated effort is often just icing on the cake. If you acquire real estate at the right time and with a soundly negotiated balance between risk and profit, time and location will do most of the work for you. Your personal effort will usually contribute to the success, but it's the nature of real estate to provide financial protection normally missing in small businesses and other types of investments.

Buying at the right time in the right location is the best thing you can do to speed up your success. A wise decision along these lines is worth more than a little time and effort. One of the most successful and well-respected real estate brokers I've had the honor of working with has a valuable expression that summarizes this idea: "Real estate success is being in the right place at the right time." The fortunate part of this truism is that there are so many right places that by just being around long enough, you're likely to hit some of them. Of course, you have to be able to recognize when you're there, and that's not always easy. Just being in real estate is not enough. However, I know a broker who might not agree with this. He made a $100,000 commission by being on floor duty when a cash-flush rancher just happened to call.

You can't "buy the real estate market" any more than you can buy the Dow Jones averages. You can only buy specific property, just as you can only buy specific stocks. Money, success, wealth, security, or whatever your objective is, can only be found (or lost) on specific real estate deals. Just getting into real estate is not the answer; it's just the first step. You must get into the right property at the right time in the right location for *you*.

After establishing your positions, coincidence may indeed work to your favor. Certainly, chance is on your side with real estate.

We live in a world of economic swings. Real estate ownership can be a way to profit from and to smooth out these extremes. It's a path open to all, without exclusion.

WHY REAL ESTATE OWNERSHIP IS AN ECONOMIC NECESSITY FOR MOST OF US

Generally speaking, there are three reasons to set up an investment program: To live comfortably now, to have the funds to live comfortably later, and to leave an estate. Building an estate is primarily a matter of a financial security that seems to become more difficult as we become a more prosperous nation. Although life has never been better or held more promise, the frustrating effects of inflation are increasing the challenge. Concern over this fact of economic progress has combined with an unprecedented credit expansion to create an explosive growth in demand for investment real estate. Real estate has been discovered as one of the few effective inflation hedges.

The realization of the important role of real estate in fighting inflation can come at the strangest times. One of my real estate friends was weaving his way through an IRS audit when he got on this subject with the agent, a man two years from retirement. Innocently, the agent started complaining about continual rent increases and how he wouldn't be able to make do after retirement. Inflation applies to all of us, even those who administer the very government spending and collection agencies that may ultimately prove to be at the root of the problem.

Taxes, to a very large degree, actually cause inflation. If you define taxes as costs imposed by government, which filter down through the economy as businesses pass the expense to customers, you can get a more accurate perspective of the problem. Taxes are often hidden, such as with social security "contributions," and even more buried within the expense of government regulations—like the legal fees required for compliance with certain Securities and Exchange Commission (SEC) matters, or the safety requirements imposed on small businesses. It's only when these many, often subtle, costs of the government's public policy cut into our take-home pay in the form of taxes and inflation that the seriousness becomes apparent.

There is a type of push-pull relationship between inflation and taxation that involves everyone who earns money or has an income and pays taxes. The more you earn, the higher the percentage of your income that goes to taxes. Our progressive tax system was originally intended by Congress to minimize taxes at lower income levels so basic needs could be met and to maximize taxes at higher levels where primary needs were not a concern. The problem today is that basic needs cost more, yet the progressive income tax structure permits you to retain an increasingly smaller percentage of each additional dollar of income, thus reducing needed income.

Although you may earn more each year, the combined effect of higher taxes and reduced purchasing power due to inflation may actually lower your standard of living.

It is generally thought that doctors are wealthy people. I accepted this modern myth until I met one who had recently been divorced. He had made a lump-sum alimony payment, which was not tax deductible, and made monthly child support payments. He was paying rent on an apartment (no deduction), supporting a car, and owned no real estate. A high before-tax income had put him in very serious financial trouble, and he was borrowing to pay income taxes. Inflation, a nondeductible life style, and a high tax bracket took away money intended for basic needs and forced him into debt. In the eyes of the IRS he was a single, high-income, high-tax bracket wage earner who paid 45% of his income in taxes. It took some fast real estate acquisition and debt restructuring to reverse the problem—he was literally going broke. It's what you keep that makes you wealthy, not what you make.

HOW TO MEASURE *YOUR* INVESTMENT RETURN AFTER TAXES AND INFLATION

To measure the profit of any investment realistically you must account for the erosion of inflation and the costs of taxation. These two factors must be treated as expense items to arrive at a return in terms of real after-tax dollars. Real dollars are dollars that represent purchasing power after inflation. The bench mark is the point in time when you make the initial investment. The object is to measure the net money you receive from that specific investment in a certain time period. To do this accurately you must determine what was earned after subtracting taxes and inflation.

A real after-tax return is simple to calculate. First subtract the tax you paid, then deduct the compounded cost of inflation during the investment holding period. The amount you have left is what the investment earned (or lost) in terms of net purchasing power. This is the true growth of your capital.

If you receive 10% interest on a $1000 bond when the inflation rate is a low 6% a year, you have 4% left in real income before taxes. If your effective tax rate is 40%, the remaining 4% will be paid in tax. Here is the calculation for a one-year holding period.

Received 10% interest on $1000 bond	$100
Less tax 40% tax bracket × $100 interest	− 40
Less inflation 6% real dollar loss × $1000 bond	− 60
Net real after-tax earnings	$ 0

With this type of debt investment, you are fighting just to stay even, as your capital shrinks by the current rate of inflation.

Here is another common example of how taxes and inflation affect capital. Say you have a savings account which has an average balance of $1000 and pays 5½% interest. Let's say that you are in the 20% tax bracket and that inflation in the items you buy (food, clothing, and so on) is 8%. What is the value of your savings at the end of the year?

Received 5½% interest on \$1000 savings	\$55
Less tax 20% tax bracket × \$55 interest	−11
Less inflation 8% real dollar loss × \$1000 savings	−80
Net real after-tax earnings (loss)	(\$36)

Vary the numbers and figure the actual effect of taxes and inflation on your investments. Try a 15% inflation rate. The steps are the same. In fact, you can determine the current percentages for taxes and inflation and calculate your real net income, whether from investments or salary. Awareness of the effect of taxes and inflation on *your* investments is the first step toward changing the situation.

To appreciate the truly unique benefits of real estate, all you need to do is learn to calculate the net *real* after-tax earnings of your capital regardless of where it is invested.

REAL ESTATE IS A HEDGE AGAINST UNCERTAINTY

The four major benefits of real estate each protect you against future economic uncertainty:

1. Cash flow offsets a temporary job loss;
2. Equity build-up acts as savings;
3. Appreciation is a buffer against inflation; and
4. Tax shelter of current income by depreciation of improvements is built-in protection against the future costs of government.

All work together to increase the probability of a financially successful investment.

Simply stated, real estate is a good business to be in. Its unique benefits provide more opportunity for financial protection and security than you may have thought possible. The relatively unrestricted allowance for initiative provides for opportunities as well as risks, but the risks are really no different from those in other investments. The rewards are much greater and in most cases far outweigh the measurable risks.

Income produced by property is just one of the components of total value. Land appreciation is another plus. Depreciation of the improvements and the resulting tax savings can also be viewed as a value benefit. Each factor must be evaluated separately, then combined to arrive at a decision about the appropriateness of a specific property for you. Often this process requires a decision concerning risks in relation to the offsetting potential for profit. First protect yourself by negotiating terms to compensate for the maximum potential loss. Then consider the greatest gain and negotiate the transaction in the hopes of achieving it. When you have explored the extremes and planned for them, you've set the stage for reasonable expectations, which is all we can realistically anticipate.

2

Putting Real Estate In Perspective

Although investment real estate is owned by many people who have no formal business education, it is a truly serious business.

Jobs produced by housing construction and real estate-related manufacturing and retail sales form an essential component of our economy. The financial benefits of new home construction and the resulting sales of appliances, carpets, and furniture filter down through the entire economic system.

When building is booming the economy is booming. When building slows, it often leads the way for recession. Working like a lead anchor it drags down employment and consumer spending, and even deflates our sense of national well-being.

HOW SUPPLY AND DEMAND WORK FOR YOUR SUCCESS

It is the fluctuation of supply and demand that creates the market in real estate. These two forces continually demonstrate their dominance throughout all aspects of our economy; the investor who doesn't learn how these basic economic forces work eventually ends up in trouble.

An understanding of how the balance shifts between supply and demand at different times in different locations can greatly increase your opportunity for success with investment real estate.

Not long ago, hundreds of "residential" and "commercial" lots were arbitrarily created out of cattle ranches in New Mexico and Arizona, and sold in New York and New Jersey. When many of the "investors" grew tired of making the payments and tried to cash in, they found that there were no buyers: there was a growing supply of lots but no natural demand. In fact, the supply and the demand had been created by out-of-town promoters. It was the local Realtors in the Southwest (whom the owners contacted in an attempt to take their nonexistent profit) who had to explain the economic facts of the market to the hapless investors. Some of these land sales operations are evolving into healthy growing communities, but it has taken time.

Learning the distinction between promotionally generated artificial demand and the natural demand of an established growing community is mandatory for safe real estate investment. You can tell the difference by looking at what is behind the market activity. Is it the natural demand for real estate resulting from solid business and population growth or is it the artificial demand of promotion? One is an opportunity for profit; the other is at best a long wait.

NATURAL DEMAND CAN TURN INTO BLIND SPECULATION

Natural demand compressed into a short time span often attracts over-speculation that produces the "bigger fool" syndrome. Buyers pay more than the property is worth in the hope that it can be sold at a profit to the next wave of speculators. The problem here is obvious for the end buyer. Whom is he going to sell to?

Although many make large profits by getting in and out of an overheated speculative demand situation, the ultimate end is the bursting of the bubble. After the stampede is over and the market collapses (often below reasonable value), prices eventually return to a more rational fluctuation between supply and demand.

There is a long history of speculative excess in all types of investment markets, from land sales to tulip bulbs. When it gets out of hand in real estate though, it can be extremely dangerous because of the large amounts of debt and long time period necessary for the market to heal. It's not uncommon for an oversupply of property (following an evaporation of demand) to be on the market for years.

Real estate market fluctuations cannot be put in proper perspective unless you consider the time factors involved. It may indeed be the case that a community begun as a land sales promotion will grow to a city of 100,000 happy residents; but when? Until that day approaches don't count on a steady demand other than that generated by the commissioned sales force. It may indeed be true that there is a continuing housing shortage, but that does not justify an irrational speculative boom based on the hope that prices have no ceiling and the fear that you may be left out.

Value adjustments resulting from shifts in supply and demand can make investment timing crucial. Initial demand has a way of leveling off and going through a period of consolidation and rest before continuing upward movement. Unfortunately, it is common for a large supply of property to come onto the market at about the time demand slows down.

This resting period in a generally growing real estate market can be an excellent entry point. It is possible to pick up property at reasonable prices, if not bargain prices, if builders are seriously overextended on construction loans. In some markets it seems almost a bargain just to find a reasonable price and solid yield, but markets have a way of changing with time.

REAL ESTATE INVESTMENT SUCCESS IS TIME DEPENDENT

Time and location determine value. Questions of "when" and "where" are of equal importance in setting up an acquisition strategy. Investors who don't ask "when" and blindly accept "where" are potential owners of desert lots.

It takes time for the natural growth of demand to build solid real estate wealth. Careful, steady acquisition of property is much more profitable financially and psychologically than being caught up in the dangers of speculative greed and risking a wipeout.

Real estate markets are inevitably defined in terms of location and time. "It is a seller's market in Houston" expresses very simply that there are more buyers than sellers there at that time. Sellers have greater control over the negotiations and price decisions.

"There is a buyer's market in Pittsburgh," of course, means the opposite: more people want to sell than buy, and buyers have the upper hand in negotiations. Ironically, though, the best time to buy is just when a market is coming out of a prolonged slump. Tomorrow's crisis forms the base from which next year's millions will be earned.

Change is the only constant in a free market. Opportunity wouldn't exist without it. Our past (and future) monetary crises and depressions have built foundations for greater economic strength and have proven to be excellent buying times for long-term real estate acquisition.

Regardless of what happens in the future, your main task is to be aware that some change will occur and that there is a natural tendency for all markets to seek a rational balance between extremes. If you know what's happening, you can learn techniques designed to work in all types of real estate markets that will help you meet your personal and financial objectives.

The opportunity for real estate acquisition is as varied as the location of property. It's all around us. When to buy is much easier to decide than where. Often, we seem to have little choice concerning timing. I know a broker who always says "buy it" if he is asked to give an opinion about a property that is fundamentally sound. He says he has never made a mistake advising a purchase when the basic value is there—but he learned the hard way. He lost some clients by being too cautious, so now his theory is that your chances are better doing something than doing nothing, provided the property meets your needs and has limited risk. It's hard to argue with that type of reasoning.

When real estate is booming it seems that *now* is the last chance to buy because you won't be able to afford the higher prices that are "sure to come." But who really knows what the future holds? Whatever it is, no investment should be made without a reasonable limit on your risk and a rational expectation of profit. Making a decision as to "where" you want to acquire real estate can be as easy as walking out your front door, and with the right negotiation techniques, "when" can be anytime you choose.

GEOGRAPHIC FLEXIBILITY EXPANDS OPPORTUNITY

Location of the real estate you acquire will, to a large degree, determine the amount of your profit. Your ability to time and negotiate the acquisition is also very important, but nothing compares with choosing the right location for lowering risk and increasing profit.

Location can refer to anything from a building site in New York to the entire Sunbelt. In choosing where to invest, try not to limit yourself. It is your decision and you should give due consideration to your own state, city, neighborhood, and city block, as well as the potential rental house next door.

Unfortunately, the choice of investment location is too often limited by unwillingness to place money out of town. Finding quality investment property is difficult anyway. Try to keep from holding yourself back because of geography. Diversity of location is a major component of real estate opportunity and it should not be viewed as a problem.

You may feel that you can only invest in familiar locations. Starting with the house next door may be a sound beginning—if it's for sale and can show a profit. You may find the details of management easier when your investment is nearby, but proximity can also be a source of trouble when tenants have easy access to you.

An acquisition strategy limited to familiar surroundings is a logical and relatively comfortable beginning, but it must take a secondary position to the economics of the market. Why pass up a profit because it is out of town? Just build in a factor for time and travel.

Some of the best buys are overlooked because of distance. It is easy to read the paper each day and check out the ads but it takes some work and extra effort to establish contacts out of town and keep in touch until a willing seller turns up. A very successful businessman who specializes in ranch acquisition proved the importance of geographic flexibility to me. He traveled throughout the Southwest by pickup to manage his diverse holdings. The more he drove, the more he acquired. The travel eventually became so extensive and his holdings so large that he bought a plane to speed up his travel and increase the time he could spend managing his property. After a couple of years he realized that he was missing the good buys by literally flying over them. He went back to driving his pickup and to visiting with his friends along the way, and his opportunities for trading real estate started growing again. The more he traveled and stayed in contact with friends, the more opportunities he found.

In today's market many of the reasonable buys never reach the open market. Consequently, your friends and contacts become very important to your success. A casual mention of someone who's thinking of selling should never be ignored. It may turn out to be your investment project for next year.

If you are hesitant about looking out of your own town, consider starting with the one-hour rule: If you can get there in one hour, it's close enough. Owning apartments an hour's drive or an hour away by air is practically like being in your own back yard. If a serious problem comes up, you can be there in short order. With competent local management, living far away can even be a benefit—you don't get the calls on Saturday night if the sewer backs up. Don't pass up a good buy because of distance, but do consider time. The location may be economically good and the distance may be inconvenient, but when time and travel costs are negotiated into the acquisition terms, the profit may make the distance shrink fast.

The primary decision criteria must be the benefits the property holds for you. Everything else is simply less important. It may in fact be that for you the distance of a certain property outweighs the benefits of ownership.

The only limit to the distance of an investment acquisition should be your ability to manage it comfortably at a profit. Even then distance is not necessarily the deciding variable. Just being familiar with a certain city may be all you need. Develop a willingness to go where the best locations are.

I once met an investor from Boston who was on his way to close the purchase of a 40-unit apartment complex in Denver. He already owned 20 units, which he had acquired while living in Denver two years earlier. He was comfortable with owning real estate in Denver, although it was a couple of thousand miles from where he lived. The economics of the property made the distance secondary. This investor really knew what he was doing. He had a computer printout on the property he was acquiring, which projected a discounted cash-flow analysis (with a very high rate of return) for the next ten years.

There are probably many solid opportunities nearby that can be acquired with the right combination of negotiation techniques. If you have time to acquire them all, you may find you've made enough money to travel on vacation instead of searching for property.

Nevertheless, with growing national affluence, easy credit, and a more sophisticated investing public, the search and competition for real estate can often be a frustrating process. This places greater responsibility on you to build value into the terms of the acquisition. Negotiation skill and knowing the right combination of techniques will play an important role in your success.

Value is not absolute, nor is it readily apparent. It is what you can do with the property that often makes it worth the price.

Different people see different opportunities at different prices. One Texas investor bought a vacant building that no one in Santa Fe would touch and turned it into one of the most successful small shopping malls in town. Being from out of town, he saw profit possibilities where local investors only saw another run-down building. He actually had seen a similar project in a different state and simply applied the idea to what was for him, "out of town."

USING TIME TO YOUR ADVANTAGE

Buying in the right location is not quite enough. You must buy at the right time. Your acquisition decisions must fully consider the effect of time on location and their combined effect on your investment return. Market values are not determined in a vacuum. They are determined by the effect of supply and demand in a specific location during a specific time period.

Not all good locations are good at all times. Time provides opportunity. Location provides opportunity. It's up to you to recognize the combination of time and location that will meet your objectives.

Real estate markets, and business in general, tend to move in cycles. A well-timed acquisition in the business cycle will help. Entry at the wrong point in time can be miserable, if not downright costly. The rule is to buy low and sell high, but how do you know when?

Answers to a few questions can help you decide. Has growth in this location just started? When did it start? Has this town been through a boom-bust cycle before? When? How long will the growth continue? When might it end? When will the consolidation period occur? Will supply catch up with demand and wash out a few builders (a common occurrence)? Where do you want to be invested if a slowdown occurs and what level of risk protection do you need to ride out temporary corrections in the supply-demand struggle?

Being aware of the timing possibilities goes a long way toward maximizing your profit and minimizing your risk. Seeing the potential of a "down-and-out" area may give you financial security faster than many obviously booming markets. There are both dangers in a boom and profits in a bust.

Our economy has more than a one-hundred-twenty-year history of rhythmic expansion and contraction, averaging about fifty-one months from low to low. Behind an increase in the number of families, which would seem to indicate greater housing demand, lurks the danger of excessive credit expansion and an inflationary blow-off, ending in a severe economic contraction. Cycle fluctuations have always been with us and probably always will be to some degree. Economic peaks and troughs should not be feared. You can adjust to them and learn to profit. They are helpful timing indicators and form the basis for investment opportunity.

THE HOUSING SHORTAGE IS REAL

There is a genuine housing shortage. It is the result of an imbalance between supply and demand that has grown out of the increase in the house-buying age population. The imbalance and demand-pull force on housing prices tend to become more severe as credit eases and as inflation fears accelerate purchases within the business cycle.

During one of the cycles a first-time real estate speculator planned and carried out a rental acquisition, programmed in advance to yield 100% in one year. He actually exceeded his objective, as many sellers do who take advantage of time-wise investment planning.

Real estate investment shows signs of becoming the only chance most people have to own a share of America. It is fast replacing the stock market in the eyes of much of the investing public. As more people become aware of the benefits (if not necessity) of owning real estate, chances are that demand for investment property will continue steadily for years to come. Regardless of credit availability and the ups and downs of the economy, strong underlying housing demand must accompany a growing population.

All the strength and prosperity of the country won't prevent an occasional and sometimes predictable economic contraction. These slumps will probably prove to be exceptional buying opportunities at a time when most will fear to invest. A rational perspective requires balanced expectations. But when the recessions pass, and growth and prosperity seem too good to end, and everyone is overly optimistic, it is time for caution.

REAL ESTATE CAN COST TOO MUCH

Nothing in the economy is forever. Inflation carries the seeds of deflation. Economic expansion has always been followed by economic contraction. Long cycles (fifty to fifty-four years) contain these somewhat regular up and down patterns and form the history of our national prosperity and well-being.

To expect prices to continue soaring forever can result in dangerous investment decisions. To expect a depression to continue forever is equally useless. Extreme inflation is an opportunity to sell at top dollar. A depression is an opportunity to buy at bottom dollar.

The challenge in any investment trend is to learn to participate profitably regardless of the direction. This requires restraint when most people are optimistic and aggressiveness when most are pessimistic. You must acquire something to sell as the market is topping and you need to conserve your cash and credit to buy as the market bottoms. Of course there is plenty of opportunity between the extremes and with an awareness of economic fluctuations you can decrease your risk and increase your profit.

When you are faced with an irrational market dominated by speculation and there seems to be no property to buy, keep in mind that eventually there will be a change. Although houses and income property are viewed as a solid hedge against inflation, there always is a price at which the public will view real estate as too expensive. Prices will then level off or drop to more reasonable levels. The dream of an investment that produces overnight fortunes has a way of eroding our more reasonable tendencies. But reality catches up when the monthly mortgage payment has to be made and the income to pay it just isn't there.

Nothing illustrates this fact better than the case of the vacant land owner who suddenly realizes that the monthly payments are competing with payment of normal living expenses. Only then is it discovered that no one seems to want to buy the land at the same tidy profit that had been planned on by the former friend who handled the purchase.

In one sad case a widower purchased several hundred acres at a price that was above the actual market: his daughter was married to the listing salesman, who needed the commission. One year after the acquisition, things changed. The daughter was divorced. The widower had borrowed against stocks to make the monthly payments and the stock market was dropping, forcing the bank to call for more collateral. Although he tried to sell on several occasions, no buyers were to be had at even a no-profit price. The private mortgage holder (seller) would not return phone calls or consider renegotiating the loan payments. Foreclosure seemed inevitable.

It is especially easy to make a bad buy when things are booming and it is equally difficult to get out when the market turns down. The problem is that in real estate the process takes years and people have short memories. An investment should be made only on its own merits, not on the blind trust of relatives, friends, or in-laws, or in the hope of finding a bigger fool to sell to later.

One of the ironic realities of the investment world is the tendency people have to buy when it's time to sell and sell when it's time to buy. This sometimes tragic curiosity is highly visible in the stock market. It seems a new generation of investors continually comes of age and goes through the initiation rites. There is a surge of buying as a bull market tops out, often forcing prices up to the point that literally exhausts demand, followed by a reversal as prices simply fall from lack of buyers. We forget that higher prices *eventually* serve to increase supply and decrease demand.

This ritual no doubt has prompted a sure-fire guideline for successful investment: Buy low and sell high. Being a cliché doesn't make it untrue; it is just not very helpful. The difficult part is determining *when* the low is reached and the high is forming.

Obviously, the crucial investment element is time, a factor which weighs heavily in favor of real estate. Real estate offers greater opportunity for profit because it's difficult to make a mistake when you use basic common sense. There is greater margin for error in timing and when a mistake is made, there is usually a graceful way out. Real estate is relatively forgiving; quite often all you have to do is buy and wait for prices to catch up if you make a mistake.

Nevertheless, real estate is not exempt from the universal laws of price movement that flow from the relationship between supply and demand. Nor are real estate investors blessed with gifts of vision unknown to, say, investors in the stock market. Even in real estate there is a greater willingness to buy and sell along with the rest of the crowd. Speculative excesses are just as dangerous in real estate as they are in the stock market, but the consequences can be more damaging because of the important role of real estate in our economy.

In real estate it is possible to fall into this trap yet survive with a profit. In the stock and financial markets it is just hard to survive, period. In both arenas the big money is dreamed about at the extremes and the realistic smart money is probably more often made in the middle. Extremes seem filled with risk, and consequently, it is only natural to fear taking action; ironically, the extremes in values are the best opportunities.

The best real estate buys are at the bottom of recessions. The problem is that money is at its tightest then and no one seems to want to let go of the little cash they may have left. That is when there are more sellers than buyers—the ideal situation for negotiating the most favorable acquisition terms.

In a way it is easier to buy when money is plentiful and credit is loose, during periods when prices are being forced to the top, testing the buying stamina of a booming market; but that's the signal to convert to cash and wait. It is definitely the time to lower your risk and pull back (lightening your debt burden) and consider the wisdom of entering a market where prices are exceeding values.

Sell when everyone wants to hold. Buy when everyone else is afraid to, not because prices are necessarily lower than two years ago, but because you have better control of the negotiations and can build in more of a profit, and reasonably limit your risk. You can negotiate better terms when the owner does not want the property anymore. Your ability to control the negotiation tends to be limited when the owner thinks he's sitting on a gold mine.

General market conditions don't necessarily make a specific property a bad buy. There is a middle ground where reasonable people can meet and set up a reasonable deal regardless of the state of the economy. When the seller can take or leave the deal, you give up a little in risk protection now and profit down the road.

Even when general market conditions don't provide the advantages you would like, there are techniques to turn the deal in your direction. You can take certain steps to structure any transaction to your advantage, to smooth out the worst possible effects, and to maximize the potential benefits.

You may think a certain property is not for you; the buyer may want too much money up front and the location may seem bad. But before you write off the deal, ask yourself what you can do to change the property and the terms of the offer. As the competition for investment property increases, the necessity for creative negotiation will become more important. Each investment opportunity should be carefully analyzed and negotiated before going to the next. Thorough analysis, skillful negotiation, and rational expectations are the foundation of successful real estate acquisition.

3

How To Minimize Risk And Maximize Profit

There is really only one question that should govern the decision to acquire a particular real estate investment: What is the probability of earning a certain profit in a given time period?

All the details of analysis and market research work toward accurately answering this question. Of course, there are many other less quantifiable and more emotional reasons for deciding to acquire certain property. One investor said his mother didn't trust buildings that weren't made out of brick, and since she was lending him the down payment, he couldn't look at apartments that weren't brick. Or, sometimes we have personal reasons of identity associated with the property we choose. Pride of ownership probably has a greater inflationary effect on investment real estate than loose credit. For example, consider the following statement, "I'm not interested in that type of property and no one that I would be associated with is either." In this case, it did not matter that the return was 25% and that there was full occupancy; it was on the wrong side of the tracks.

Sometimes it is not monetary reward or financial risk that has the last word. Too often emotion outweighs financial gain and the outcome is a purchase at the top of the market and a ticket for a ride to the bottom. It is this emotional factor that should be carefully considered prior to any investment commitment. Certainly, you must buy what you want, but people who buy for emotional reasons often end up in trouble.

Putting the personal aspects aside, there is only the relationship between profit and loss that governs the financial benefits of real estate investment. During the question period following a speech on the real estate market, a very concerned woman asked me how anyone could buy apartments when there seemed to be so many under construction and advertised in the paper for rent. My answer reiterated the importance of the relation between supply and demand. A seemingly large supply doesn't necessarily mean high risk when the demand is there. The new supply of apartments was being steadily absorbed by an expanding population. Housing needs were growing in leaps and bounds, rents had increased to a profitable level in spite of high interest rates, and developers were trying to catch up with demand. And as the new units came on line, ads were placed in the paper as part of the rent-up phase. Certainly, there were more units, but there were more renters too, and occupancy was at 98%. Supply and demand were both growing, but demand was growing faster and the supply wasn't likely to catch up for a couple of years.

COMMON SENSE INVESTMENT ANALYSIS

There are a couple of basic questions that are worth careful consideration before making a commitment to any real estate investment. They are really just common sense questions and can be answered at the level of detail appropriate for you. The first question deals with profit potential.

1. Will the future cash flows exceed the expenses by a satisfactory amount? It is difficult to forecast the future, but an attempt to project past performance into a *reasonable range* of expectations is basic to all business, including real estate investment.

Lay out the property's past performance and project it into the future. The key to accuracy is completeness. Compare pre-tax and after-tax income. Take a close look at all expenses and the effect of inflation. It is especially important with real estate to consider the net proceeds when you sell. Making a profit when you sell is as much a part of cash flow as monthly operating profit—it just happens to come in a lump sum later on.

If you want to go even further in your analysis, discount all the future cash flows and investments by the anticipated rate of inflation and determine your real percentage return on investment (in purchasing power).

The second question deals with risk—the ever-present uncertainty of all investments.

2. *What are the chances that you're wrong and what do you do if you are?* It makes plain good sense to have contingency plans. Protection can often be negotiated into the acquisition terms, such as no personal liability and partial release clauses in the case of vacant land. Although the sky's the limit, there is nothing like a safe exit for a good night's sleep. Plan for maximum profit, but negotiate risk protection into the deal in case circumstances you can't possibly foresee shoot down your projections.

Realistically, the most likely outcome will prove to be on reasonable middle ground somewhere between your most optimistic dreams and worst fears. Mapping out the possibilities in advance and even quantifying their effect on your rate of return can go a long way toward ensuring that what you plan is what actually happens. You may even discover that the danger that concerns you the most would have little or no effect on the project's overall rate of return. I know one investor who was hung up on trying to determine whether or not the hot water heaters were about to blow up. His major interest when analyzing apartment units was the amount of water heaters that had been replaced. If the water heaters were too old for him he wouldn't buy the apartments. The sad thing about this is that he wouldn't accept that: (1) the possibility of replacement was uncertain, and (2) even if a significant number had to be replaced over the period of his ownership, the effect on his return would be negligible.

When you learn to quantify your concerns you take a large step toward common sense. If you hesitate to take action because of a problem you anticipate, try to reduce the problem to a range of costs, then plug the figures into your projections and really see if the effect on your rate of return will be significant.

It's learning to combine common sense with cool mathematical analysis that will separate you from the unsuccessful emotional buyers. You may see potential overlooked by the seller as well as by other investors. It may just turn out to be your insight and hard work that make a sound income out of what others have seen as a high risk and potential loss. The one thing in real estate that can hold you back is failure to rely on your own common sense judgment.

AVOID THE HIGH DOWN PAYMENT—LOW RISK MYTH

The possibility of financial loss is not eliminated by making a large down payment. Profit is not necessarily assured either. Although most people associate a large equity with safety, the reality of the matter is that the more money you commit, the more you have to lose if things go against you.

Making a high profit with little risk of loss is the product of knowledge and good judgment, not money. I know one investor who had a sound and effective strategy that served his acquisition program well. Over a period of approximately eight years he acquired property valued at more than ten million dollars. He began with no money but he was a whiz at math. He did it entirely through his skill as a negotiator.

His technique was effective and simple. It was a combination of shrewd negotiation, analysis ability, and good management. It began with a purchase agreement that was contingent on a refinancing of the property in an amount large enough to pay the existing loans and to meet the down payment requirements of the seller. The negotiation key involved convincing the seller to carry a portion of his equity on a second mortgage.

He would offer to purchase a complex, such as the American West Apartments, with a $475,000 down payment, provided he could arrange a new first mortgage and the seller would carry a second mortgage for the difference between the purchase price and the new first mortgage. Often he was able to negotiate the price down and the property appraisal and new loan up. This, of course, reduced the amount of the second mortgage. Occasionally he would divert part of the new loan proceeds to do major repairs on the apartments. This increased the second mortgage.

AMERICAN WEST APARTMENTS

Original Terms		*Acquisition Structure*	
Price	$1,300,000	Price	$1,300,000
Existing Loan	−500,000	New Mortgage	−975,000
Equity	−800,000	Second Mortgage	−325,000
Balance	−0−	Balance	−0−

There is a mathematical requirement that must be met in order for this technique to work. The existing mortgage must be lower than the current loan value by an amount large enough to pay it off and satisfy the seller's need for cash. This means that the appraisal of the property, for purposes of the new loan, must be high enough to generate the cash necessary to pay off the existing loan and still leave at least enough for a down payment satisfactory to the seller. Therefore, the old loan ($500,000) and the down payment ($475,000) equal the new loan ($975,000). The sales price ($1,300,000) is the sum of the new loan and the second mortgage. The seller's equity ($800,000) is the total of the down payment and the second mortgage.

This investor always included a clause in the purchase contract that required all costs of closing to be taken from the new loan proceeds and that any costs he owed were to be added to the second mortgage. He acquired property without any money of his own. In fact, he often pulled cash out as a result of prorations and appraisals that were higher than his purchase price.

Lenders often look favorably on projects that a developer can put together with skill alone. One mortgage broker put it this way: "Lenders respect a developer who can put a project together without any of his own money. It shows that he knows what he's doing."

And that's the key—knowing what you're doing.

THE MYTH AND REALITY OF LOSING PROPERTY

Income property should always stand on its own merits, not upon the financial statement of the investor. This operating principle is fundamental to avoiding the "bigger fool" trap of irrational speculation. The success of a real estate investment is not insured by a large down payment, nor is it necessarily endangered by a small down payment. The net income-producing ability of the property now and in the future is the measure of its financial success, and this can often be assured by means other than a large cash outlay.

It may take a large down payment or it may take none at all to gain control of a certain property. Your negotiation of the acquisition will decide the basic degree to which you are in control and will establish the initial financial projections. Then your management ability will be called upon to keep costs down and income steady, and to determine whether your initial plan can become a reality. The amount of down payment is often a function of the seller's emotions rather than of the financial requirements of the project. This emotional aspect can be a benefit for you because of the opening it provides for negotiation.

If the property you're trying to acquire gives off signals that indicate future foreclosure, then something may be wrong with the deal. It could be a problem with the property, such as location, or a problem not necessarily concerning the property itself, or even traffic flow. It might be a problem with the loan terms or it could be poor management. If you are worried about losing the property you acquire, the less down payment and personal liability the better. Consider the economics of the property, the financing, and your own management ability to ensure that foreclosure is a distant and remote possibility. Unfortunately, there are operators who try to structure impossible financing then sell to poor managers in the hopes of foreclosing later and reselling. If you make a deal with one of these characters and discover his intentions before it's too late, get out fast.

In any event, work toward structuring your investments so that you can't get seriously hurt no matter what happens to your property or the general economy. Value in real estate is ultimately determined by what you can do with it. By careful negotiation and analysis you can protect yourself against loss by never extending your commitment beyond the reasonable limits of what you and the property you acquire can do.

THE IMPORTANT ROLE OF NEGOTIATION IN ACQUISITION

Negotiation skill can, in effect, replace money, but money can never take the place of a good negotiator.

Fortunately, negotiation skill can be developed. You can learn to work with people and direct the course of events in a mutually beneficial direction. Sometimes gaining the upper hand is difficult, and in certain situations there's just no way to reach a mutually beneficial compromise. There are people who will not give an inch on their terms. It's this type of tough, seemingly unreasonable negotiator, who can teach us a few practical lessons.

Strength in negotiation is built upon giving the impression that you don't need success. It may be that you want the negotiations to succeed very much. But you gain the upper hand when it is apparent that you can quite easily walk away from the deal without the least amount of pain. You can train yourself to do this—to walk away from a deal you want when the terms are not right for you.

Even though you may have to leave a few opportunities on the table, never close the door. Walk away with this attitude: "Maybe we can talk about it later." Be interested without being needy. Develop patience. Accomplishing a worthwhile acquisition can take a long time. Develop confidence. If you miss a solid opportunity, keep in mind that you will eventually find another.

Negotiation is not necessarily an exercise in giving up terms you want. It can be a creative process of discovering alternatives, not thought of previously, which may make the deal better than originally planned.

When you are faced with the necessity of backing down on a point, it is often better to talk around it and to get the entire transaction set up before you give in. When you do give in, do it suddenly, accepting the whole deal. Structure your compromise so that it cements all aspects of the negotiation. In other words, try to work in the points you want (every one of them) as a condition of a compromise acceptance.

Never give the impression that you're willing to give in just for the sake of making the deal. Just present what works best for you as poker-faced as you can. If it is not accepted, keep pulling out alternatives until you find a combination that works. Keep negotiating in a collected and unemotional manner either until the deal fits together or you run out of alternative proposals. If it works, fine. If it doesn't work, neither give up nor give in—just say goodby and look for other property. You may even get a phone call offering a compromise better than you would have ever asked for. There is always another chance, and there always will be.

Strength in negotiation comes as much from your attitude toward yourself as it does from your attitude toward the seller. Have confidence and believe that if a certain deal falls through, you'll just go on to the next one, until you succeed.

THE MECHANICS OF BUYING

There are four general processes characteristic of most real estate acquisitions:

1. Negotiating the terms (often in writing);
2. Agreeing, in writing, to what you negotiated (signing);
3. Arranging any loans necessary; and
4. Closing the transaction.

Each step has certain routine requirements which are designed to complete a deal smoothly. Although it can be a source of comfort that much of the paper work is handled by specialists (Realtors, lawyers, escrow agents), it cannot relieve you as buyer from the responsibility of understanding what is happening every step of the way. It is your money, your property, and your responsibility to maintain control and to avoid becoming an inadvertent victim of circumstances, or worse.

The initial negotiation process is your first opportunity to gain some degree of control and to set up the transaction the way you want it. This is when the various acquisition techniques come into play. The terms reached at this point may very well determine your profit when you sell. It is the most important stage in any acquisition. From this point on it gets increasingly difficult to make changes.

Negotiation is your chance to include the techniques that will limit your risk and maximize your profit. Ask and you might get. All they can say is no. The point is that real estate acquisition starts with bargaining, known in polite circles as negotiating. No one is going to give you what you want unless you ask for it, and now is the time to ask.

The mechanics of asking requires two things:

1. Willingness to lay your position on the line during the talking stage when a meeting of the minds is in the process of forming; and
2. Close attention to detail to make sure what is agreed upon during oral negotiation becomes a written agreement.

It's very important to get a written agreement as soon as possible. Gains made during initial negotiations mean nothing if they don't end up in the written agreement. Expect nothing until you have it in writing. It's easy for misunderstanding to develop when you're talking about somewhat complex acquisition terms. Even when you have the terms clearly defined in a purchase agreement problems can come up later.

It is important to make sure that the terms of the original negotiation are actually included in the final documents. Even the best legal secretaries sometimes leave out important points that can have a direct impact on your future income.

In one transaction an unintentional omission in an important document almost reduced my cash flow by $600 per month. The purchase agreement stated that the monthly payments on the second real estate contract would increase to $1000 per month, "including interest," after the existing first mortgage was paid in full. When the final contract was typed the sentence read "$1000 per month *plus* interest"—an increased payment of over 50%. Fortunately, the sellers willingly made the necessary change when I caught the error during closing. If it had gone through undetected, in six years the escrow agent would have routinely presented a very unwelcome surprise. It would have been very difficult to correct after all the documents had been recorded and the people involved had gone their various ways.

You have to track the progress of what you agree to during negotiations and make sure that the proper documents are worded correctly. It helps to let as many eyes review for errors as possible; one more person with a fresh viewpoint may catch something previously overlooked. The purpose is not to catch someone making a mistake, but to help each other work through the transaction with as few errors as possible. When the going gets complicated, the more solution-oriented helpers the better.

When you get past the written agreements you have essentially "got a deal." Hopefully what follows is simply a routine process of carrying out the agreements. Believe it or not, there are many transactions that go through closing without a hitch.

It is normal to have problems in business, and if you have trouble dealing with them normally, consider whether you really want to set up a program of real estate acquisition. It's the calm, cool, and collected who take home the profits year after year. If you are a person who gets upset easily, plan on being unnerved regularly when you enter the real estate market.

Although you may have done some preliminary investigation, the next step involves going through the details of setting up any loans necessary for completing the acquisition. This is the one aspect of any real estate purchase that must go routinely, for a very good reason: institutional financing should be virtually assured before you sign the purchase agreement. If you have to go through the process of obtaining financing, say so in the purchase agreement and make the transaction contingent on the financing. But keep in mind that until all contingencies are met and removed from the agreement by signed acknowledgment, you don't have a solid, legally enforceable transaction.

Making the arrangements for an institutional loan, before you get into the details of negotiation, will give you an edge. You have to know how much money you have before you can negotiate from a position of strength. Whether the money is from your pocket or from a bank's vault is of no concern to the seller. You must know that you can close the deal you agree to before you start talking.

It's a different story, of course, when you are arranging for the seller to carry back a portion of his equity on a purchase money mortgage. Instead of the bank holding the mortgage, the seller does. This financing technique provides one of the greatest opportunities for negotiation and problem solving in real estate. You don't have to fight the policies of a lender and you have a chance to give-and-take a little with the seller, who also has an interest in seeing the deal go through.

Closing your acquisition should follow naturally from the written agreements. When working with an established escrow or title company, you can usually rest assured that they will do the most professional job they're capable of. If you are not working with an established escrow company, be prepared to encounter a few problems. In any event, never consider the deal final until closing has been completed and you are the owner of record.

4

Thirty-two Techniques For Acquiring Real Estate When You Don't Have Cash

Knowing the possibilities gives you the opportunity to speed up your acquisition plans. Actually applying your knowledge is up to you. If you make the effort to learn what others have done, you simply increase your chances by drawing on their knowledge. This is the purpose behind the following techniques: to give you the advantage that comes from knowing specific ways of getting the job done.

Many of the techniques will not fit your immediate needs, but someday they may. Others may solve an immediate problem and pave the way for closing an acquisition that you've had your eye on for some time. In any event, the objective is to give you the widest possible range of alternatives to choose from. Look at these techniques as the starting point. They are meant to be modified. Try to combine and customize them to fit your specific needs.

MORTGAGE OUT

Mortgaging out is probably the most sought-after objective of builder-developers. Meeting this increasingly elusive objective requires a combination of cost control and solid income tenants. Developers have found mortgaging out increasingly difficult as land and construction costs have increased. However, rents have also climbed, so with a shrewd approach you can still build value into certain projects successfully.

By definition, you mortgage out when the permanent loan is equal to or larger than your total acquisition costs. The mathematical key is to keep land and construction costs at the same percentage of appraised value as the financing. With existing projects the sales price must equal the loan value of the property.

If your rents are high enough to generate an appraisal based on income that is comfortably above your costs, you are in business. Since lenders base their estimate of value on the income-producing ability of the property, you have a built-in chance. Everything from ranches to shopping centers have been acquired using this technique.

The objective is to keep costs of land and construction to about 70% or 80% of appraisal, depending on the percentage of value you will receive from the loan. Investors who have an inventory of commercial land acquired years ago have a definite advantage. Land that was acquired just a few years ago will probably contribute to an appraised value far in excess of its original cost. But there are a couple of other alternatives if land costs are a problem in your area.

A carefully negotiated long-term land lease with low payments at the outset may give you the margin for borrowing the initial development money you need. Another alternative involves working in small towns before land values climb out of sight. Big name, grade A tenants and a shopping center developer-builder who can leave his profit in the project can add to the ease of mortgaging out.

REFINANCE WITH THE SELLER CARRYING BACK A SECOND

This technique is a natural for acquiring older property (especially apartments) that can be refinanced. The primary objective of this approach is to obtain a new first mortgage large enough to pay both the existing loans and the down payment required by the seller. The down payment actually comes from the proceeds of the new first mortgage.

The balance of the sales price is then carried by the seller on a second mortgage. It may also be possible for you to structure the terms of the transaction so that a portion of the loan proceeds are used for renovation of the property. The proceeds of the new loan, therefore, can meet three objectives: to pay the existing loans, to pay the down payment, and to upgrade the property.

As with most acquisition techniques, this one works smoothly when the seller wants out and trusts your management ability. The challenge here is to make the seller accept a totally financed acquisition. Of equal importance is the necessity of building enough value into your loan presentation to get the largest possible first mortgage. This requires a very complete presentation of the changes you will make in the property, the benefits of the management system you will implement, and the steps you will take to increase the income. The objective is to convince the seller and lender that you are the best possible buyer and that their interests will be better cared for when you own the property.

There are a couple of direct benefits to the seller. He steps out of the liability of the existing loans because you have refinanced, and he gets the down payment he wants from the proceeds of the new loan. Since he was probably prepared to carry back a second position anyway, nothing has changed substantially. The main negotiating block may be over the amount of the second mortgage. But this need not be a problem if the seller has confidence in the income-producing power of the property and in your ability to manage it professionally.

CREATE PAPER

Solid real estate equity is buying power. And in times of high inflation it is a source of capital appreciation—the only type of gain that can keep your estate even with, or ahead of, inflation. Creating paper is a method of using the purchasing power of your home or other real estate equity without refinancing or selling.

The mechanics of this approach are simple. You sign a note, usually payable in monthly installments, which is secured by a second mortgage on real estate you own. The note buys out the seller's equity in the property you are acquiring. It is the down payment. If you default on the note, the seller gets your other property. As added security, the terms could be written so that in the event of default the seller would get the property he sold you as well.

Of course, you would not want to use this technique if there were the least possibility of default. The income must be there to support the payments. The use of your real estate as security can be a means of ensuring the seller that the note for the down payment will be paid.

A personal note backed with solid collateral that meets the income needs of the seller often makes more sense than a lot of cash when you calculate the tax benefits. Spreading out payment of the seller's equity spreads out the tax on his profit. Why should a seller demand a lot of cash, when receiving the cash may actually increase the total amount that passes through his hands on the way to the federal government? The only logical reason is to meet a desire for security. Using other property as security for the note can meet this need.

REFINANCE YOUR HOME

The steady, unrelenting increase in single family home values is probably the major factor contributing to the broad acceptance of real estate as an investment. The equity in your home that grows each month by paying the loan and by market value appreciation is now widely recognized as equivalent to having money in the bank. Home ownership seems to be replacing savings, often by necessity rather than by choice.

Recognition of home equity as solid security has redefined this former consumer item as an acceptable low-risk investment. Consequently, savings and loans and banks are fighting to develop new types of home loans. Cities are even entering the market by issuing bonds for inter-city home loan funds. This is an example of a political motive competing with a profit motive.

Putting the home in the spotlight increases the opportunity for more aggressive investing with equity. You can turn your equity into cash in two ways: refinance completely or add a second mortgage. The rapid increase in home values gives you a chance to put solid equity to work acquiring additional investment real estate. It also gives you a chance to become overextended. But with prudent planning and proper financial analysis, your home equity can be a safe source of investment capital.

The challenge here is to put the cash (which of course is tax-free) to work earning investment dollars. Using the refinance proceeds for consumer goods doesn't make sense, since no income or capital gain are produced to repay the debt.

The obvious requirement of this technique is that the money earned by the real estate acquired with the refinance proceeds be sufficient to offset the risk of additional debt on such an important asset as your personal residence. Carefully weigh the balance between risk and reward before using this approach.

PROFESSIONAL SERVICES AS DOWN PAYMENT

If you don't have cash, what do you have? That is the basic question to explore thoroughly as you negotiate any acquisition. Often the answer falls back on what you can do that is of benefit to the seller.

Sellers who really want out for good will often look to your management ability. Just knowing that their equity will be protected by good management and that they will eventually be paid from the improved operating efficiency of the property can be enough to swing the deal. If you can provide this kind of assurance and add another benefit, you may be in good shape.

Do you have a professional skill the seller might need that would meet part or all of the down payment requirement? For example, if the seller is interested in the stock market and you are a computer programmer, create a program to trade stocks, or perhaps, test the seller's system and manage the transactions.

Lawyers and doctors have an advantage with this technique because of the high costs of their professions; and eventually everyone needs their services. Contractors and related building professions also have an edge here because real estate sellers often have other property that may need work. This is a natural opportunity to trade for the down payment consideration.

Knowing the seller is often half the battle. If you have an idea of what he wants out of life, you may be able to jump the cash gap and go directly to his objective. There are several things any seller can do with the cash he has, whether it comes from a down payment or from his job. What can you provide as a replacement for cash?

EFFORT EQUITY

There are several applications of effort equity. It can be used to acquire a home through the Federal Housing Administration (FHA) or to acquire an interest in a partnership.

If you are putting a partnership together for real estate acquisition, a percentage of the ownership may be appropriate compensation. This is often an expected incentive built into the project from the beginning.

The FHA has a provision that allows the buyer to apply "sweat equity" to the down payment requirement. You receive credit for the labor you put into the property to bring it up to FHA standards.

The purpose of this technique is for you to receive credit, toward the down payment, for the value of the effort you contribute to the property or project. In complicated investment transactions, it is usually one person who creates the idea for a real estate transaction and puts together the final deal. Without this type of effort few deals would close. More often than not, the value of the property is enhanced as a result. When this is being done for the benefit of a partnership, it is appropriate that the creating member be compensated for the extra effort. Equity in the property is one solid form of compensation. It is also a method of ensuring a profitable investment when the partners look to the same person for the management and ultimate sale of the property.

Real estate brokers who work with out-of-town investors have an edge here. There is a degree of added comfort when you know that someone is there who will stand behind the property and work out the problems. A right to participate in ownership makes good business sense when the primary owner knows that someone else must put in some effort for his profit. The same reasoning lies behind stock option compensation for corporate executives.

BORROW AGAINST PAPER

If you own second mortgages, trust deeds, or real estate contracts secured by property previously sold, consider using them as collateral for acquisition funds.

A second mortgage is a depreciating "debt" investment. Real property is normally considered to be an appreciating "equity" investment. Borrowing against your depreciating paper to buy appreciating income property is a method of converting the asset to cash without disposing of it, thereby triggering a tax liability.

As payments are received on your paper-collateral they are applied directly to repayment of the loan. The value previously stored in the paper, which was formerly diminishing with each principal payment and with each jump in inflation, is now stored in an appreciating investment. This was achieved by borrowing against the paper to generate the cash necessary to meet the down payment requirements of the seller. The net effect of this procedure is that a portion of your capital gain is reinvested while the tax is deferred.

The amount you can borrow against secured paper will depend somewhat on your relationship with the lender. About 50% of the face value of the paper is the standard. The amount may vary upwards or downwards based on your equity and lien position. The condition and value of the property securing the paper will also be a factor. You may be able to borrow more if the property securing the paper is sound and if you have a solid position that will allow a quick discount sale in the event of default.

This technique is based on the principle of moving the value you have to the property you want. You just hitch a ride on borrowed cash to make the move.

SELLER PAYS BUYER

It may be somewhat of a surprise to you that a seller of real estate in today's market would actually pay someone to buy his property. The instances in which I have seen this happen were both rather large properties with correspondingly large debts. Sellers were anxious to escape their obligations and use their energies in more productive pursuits. Furthermore, it was going to take some cash to turn the performance of the properties around.

In some cases an overextended property owner who doesn't have the expertise or inclination to deal with real estate that is losing money can be a most willing negotiator. His cooperation can even extend to providing the cash necessary to offset the risk he is transferring to the buyer. Cases like this illustrate the fact that all real estate is not necessarily appropriate for all investors. In any event, this technique allows an owner to get out of a very bad situation.

As a practical matter, the cash advanced by the seller may, by necessity, be put back into the property to finance the changes needed to make it productive. This cash outlay by the seller is not necessarily a negotiated gift. It can also be structured as a loan secured by the acquired property. Consequently, the seller can act as lender, selling to someone who can do the job and financing his efforts to do it. There are situations in real estate, as in general business, that require an infusion of cash to operate productively. A seller who puts up money to protect his equity and other assets may be making a sound business move.

ACQUIRE WITH FUTURE PROFITS

If you are going into a project that has a doubtful cash flow, this technique may neutralize part of the risk. It is a deferred down payment method that is tied to the profitability of the property you are acquiring.

The value of the target property may be based on comparable sales and replacement cost analysis, but it may lack the income to justify the owner's equity requirement. The source of the income problem may be poor management, a lack of demand, or a mistake in the design of the property, such as inadequate parking. Regardless of the cause, you should see a ready solution before taking on the problem.

This is the type of opportunity that will allow you to negotiate your way into ownership and pay for it by virtue of your entrepreneurial and management skills. As the property begins to show a net profit above a predetermined monthly amount the seller receives payment toward his equity. Every dollar above the agreed-upon monthly minimum goes to the seller. The faster you turn the property around, the faster the seller is paid. He shares the risk by waiting for payment until the property produces.

The idea of this technique is to give you enough margin to make a losing investment a productive one without the pressure and risk of laying out a cash down payment. It is a method of making a property pay its own way while giving the right buyer an incentive to see that the job gets done.

ACQUIRE WITH CLOSING CREDITS

This is an approach that uses time to your direct advantage. It combines the mechanics of closing with planned timing to offset the net cash you must pay at closing. This technique uses routine closing calculations (often a source of surprise) to your advantage.

When you buy toward the end of the tax year, but before property taxes are due and a few days after the rent on the property is due, you are in line for certain cash benefits. Although the net effect may depend on the type of loan you're assuming, the proration of taxes and rents will usually reduce the amount of cash needed to close.

When you close after a significant portion of the year has passed during which the seller was liable for property taxes, you will be credited with the amount of the seller's tax liability. Then when the property tax bills become due, you will pay them outright for the entire year. Until the tax bills are due you have use of that money, money that can be used as a portion of the down payment.

Of equal importance is the proration of rents. When you close a few days after the rent is due, you will usually receive credit for a proportional balance of the rent representing the remaining days in the month. You own the property as of the day of closing, so you get the rent for the rest of the month. Timing your purchase and planning the routine math in your favor can significantly reduce the cash due at closing and even entirely eliminate it when combined with other techniques. Always figure out your net cash due at closing *after prorations* before deciding you don't have enough money for a down payment.

ASSIGN THE RENTS

When you are borrowing the down payment from a bank and need additional security, this approach may help. The income stream from the property you are acquiring is itself a source of security. It has value and can be used as loan collateral.

If the terms of the existing loans on the property you are acquiring do not stipulate that the rents have previously been assigned, you have made it past the first barrier. All you need is an "assignment of rents" agreement drawn by a knowledgeable real estate lawyer and a loan officer willing to accept this agreement as backup for your signature on a loan.

A properly written assignment gives the lender the right to impound rents to pay the loan in the event of default. This added security for the down payment loan may be the edge you need to satisfy your banker.

Of course, you are negotiating what is essentially a commercial signature loan, and the bank will normally look to your total financial statement and credit history in making the decision. Any form of security you can provide will simply make your chances of success that much better. By assigning the rents, you give the bank additional collateral to meet the ever-present need of satisfying bank examiners—a requirement your loan officer must always keep in mind. When you know of ways to beef up the security for your loan, you just make it that much easier for a loan officer to help you. Keep in mind that a cash-flow history and a projection on the property you are acquiring is required backup material when you are applying for a down payment loan, regardless of the security you offer.

ACQUIRE WITH A REPAIR PARTNERSHIP

Property that needs rehabilitation may be a headache for the owner but it is an opportunity for you to put together a repair partnership. Start by determining potential partners who have skills that will upgrade the property. A plumber, an electrician, a carpenter, and others can contribute their work toward the down payment. Each receives a percentage of ownership equal to the value of the work contributed. The improvements increase the property's value, thereby replacing the seller's need for some evidence that the buyers won't default.

The seller takes his equity on a purchase money mortgage and in effect has greater security, by virtue of the rehabilitation, than with a nominal cash down payment.

The work done by the partners serves as security to the seller that the buyers have put true value into the property and won't readily default on the loans. The sales price can even be negotiated upward to reflect the added value as a result of the renovation contributions, if necessary. This would increase the face amount of the purchase money mortgage.

There is also a way of determining the sales price based on the rehabilitation costs. If the work contributed by the partners represents 20% of the ultimate market value of the property after repairs, the sales price would then be 80% of that figure. Consequently, the note and mortgage to the seller is 80% of the eventual value, which may be more or less than the original asking price.

Sometimes the only way to save a property from going downhill is to bring it back up with an infusion of long-overdue repairs. A seller who realizes this may ultimately come out ahead, avoiding the serious loss that could otherwise have occurred if the deterioration of the property had not been stopped.

THE NOTE PARTNERSHIP

Several small notes signed by a number of individuals can be better security than one large note signed by one person. Ten $9,000 notes from different people, each having a net worth of $90,000, is sounder security than a note from one person with a net worth equal to the face value of the note. Acquisition partnerships that realize the negotiation advantage of buying as a group can be quite successful.

An additional advantage to this method is the flexibility it provides the seller. If cash is needed from time to time the seller can discount and sell one of the notes without stepping into a tax liability for the entire profit—installment reporting can be protected.

Security for the notes can be handled in a couple of ways. A mortgage on the acquired property could serve as security for all the notes. Another approach is to have each of the partners secure his note by a separate mortgage placed on different property owned outside the partnership. In fact, individual residences may prove to be better collateral in the eyes of the seller than the property he sold.

If the property acquired is used to secure the notes, it is important to word the documents so that a default by one partner would trigger default of the entire property. This protects the seller. The notes and mortgage should also be written to protect the other partners by giving them the right to step in and cure a default by one of the other members.

Negotiating a no-cash acquisition can sometimes be accomplished more easily by spreading the liability (and security) among several people.

ADVERTISE FOR A PRIVATE LOAN

This method of raising acquisition capital proves that you never really know what is possible until you try. Venture capital provided by individuals and privately owned companies has often been the foundation of new businesses. It is no different in real estate. One young real estate entrepreneur turned a steady credit line provided by a wise and trusting widow into a multimillion dollar company. The right kind of financial backing has helped more than one hard-working person to the top, and it can just as easily happen to you.

If you have found what seems to be one of those rare opportunities to buy that comes along when you are least prepared financially, consider advertising for a private loan. With a project that has solid potential you can offer higher than usual interest and a percentage of the profits, if necessary. You may be surprised at the response if your ad request clearly reflects the unique opportunity you perceive in the property.

There are people with money who know a good opportunity when it is presented to them and want an above-average return for their willingness to take a chance. You may already know of someone like this, or know a company that specializes in what is traditionally considered high-risk venture capital lending. If you do, it may not be necessary to advertise. But if you don't, why not try an ad?

With the general acceptance of real estate as a solid hedge against inflation, many of the difficulties of long ago are gone. People are now searching for ways to participate in the growth of real estate. One way to participate, without the management demands of direct ownership, is to lend money to people who have found a good buy.

COMMISSION AS DOWN PAYMENT

This acquisition technique illustrates one of the real benefits of being a licensed real estate agent. I have met people who have entered the real estate brokerage business mainly because of the commission benefit when they acquire property for their own account.

In some ways, being active in the real estate brokerage business is very similar to having a seat on the Stock Exchange. You are in the middle of the action and can see opportunities while they are still in the formative stage. And you can cut the cost of entry by the amount of your own fee when you buy for your own account.

Real estate commissions are generally paid in cash at closing of the transaction. The net effect of paying a commission is that both the sales price and the cash received by the seller are reduced. Conversely, when a broker invests for his own account, the net effect of receiving a commission is a reduction of both the price and cash required for down payment.

This technique is practically applied during negotiation in order to eliminate the unnecessary payment and repayment of cash between buyer and seller. There is really no need to run the commission through the hands of the escrow agent twice: from the buyer to the seller for down payment and back to the buyer in the form of commission. The obvious alternative is to agree, during negotiation, to reduce the sales price by the amount of the commission and deduct it from the cash down payment.

CREDIT UNION LOAN

If you are a member of a credit union, you have an inside track for getting an acquisition loan. Furthermore, the interest rate and terms are often easier to digest than those of the neighborhood bank.

Employee credit unions exist essentially for the benefit of the employees. If you have the good fortune of belonging to an institution that has a credit union, it should be considered one of your first sources for an acquisition loan.

The process is not unlike that of a bank. It is just easier sometimes because of the inter-relationship between the credit union, your job, and your employer. There is less risk from the credit union's point of view—they know you have a secure job.

The amount of the loan and the type of collateral, if any, will vary based on your income and the money you have on deposit with the credit union. But the point is that the credit union is there for your benefit, and using it for real estate acquisition capital is one of the best ways to realize your benefits.

REAL ESTATE EQUITY AS DOWN PAYMENT

This technique is really a form of real estate exchange and has an amazing number of very effective applications. For our purposes, though, it is useful in developing a somewhat different view of the ways you can use the real estate you now own.

Equity in real estate is one of the most effective forms of purchasing power available to investors today. It can be a tax-free, inflation resistant and a relatively liquid asset when you know the unique exchange techniques.

As you may know, when certain legal requirements are met you can exchange investment real estate for other investment real estate without paying tax on the profit. This special real estate opportunity is provided by Section 1031 of the Internal Revenue Code and has an incredible number of variations.

For example, if you have located a larger investment property that better suits your objectives than the property you now own, consider making an exchange. In effect, when you exchange, the equity in your property serves as the down payment for the property you acquire. If you receive no cash or other consideration and assume larger loans, you will pay no tax on the disposition of your original property. This tax advantage alone makes exchanging desirable in many cases—why sell and pay tax when you can exchange tax-free?

In addition, when you use exchanging to build your estate you can eliminate the need to raise cash. The erroneous objection that often discourages sound exchanges is the unfounded assumption that the owner of the property you want doesn't want your property. You never know until you try. And even if the seller won't accept your property, there is an easy and routine method of structuring an exchange for you and a sale for him. You simply enter into an agreement to exchange contingent on the sale of your property out of escrow.

Using the real estate you have to acquire the real estate you want makes good sense when the alternative is selling, paying tax, and buying with the money you have left over. For the details of practical tax-free exchanging, see my book, *Real Estate Exchange and Acquisition Techniques,* published by Prentice-Hall.

FAMILY LOAN

Don't overlook the possibility of borrowing from family members to raise the cash you need for a worthwhile investment.

How many people have been forced to borrow occasionally from close family to get through difficult times? Borrowing to acquire solid investment real estate makes a lot more sense in many ways.

When the investment opportunity is unique and is liable to slip through your fingers unless prompt action is taken, consider talking it over with the people who care about you the most. There are a lot of benefits here: no credit check, probably a fast OK, and the loan application can probably be made over the dinner table. And you may actually be doing a family friend a favor by providing good security and higher interest than a savings account.

The point here, as with all acquisition techniques, is that you must consider all funding alternatives and combinations of alternatives; borrowing from your family is one of the most often used and most often successful choices you can make.

ACQUISITION WITH SOFT PAPER

Soft paper refers to loans that have low initial payments. The terms can be structured for interest only at the beginning, with an increased principal reduction later. The term of the loan is also lengthened in certain cases to meet the objective of this technique, which is to "soften" the impact of the payments on the buyer. Therefore, when you acquire real estate with soft paper, the transaction is set up to make the monthly payments easier for you.

High prices have forced many lenders to accept longer term financing for new car loans as well as for government-sponsored and conventional home mortgages. This continuing institutional trend has made the use of soft paper more easily accepted in real estate negotiations. In the past, soft paper was used on purchase money mortgages when prices ran up and credit tightened. Now it is the only way many people can afford a car or home.

Soft paper allows you to acquire the property you want, even when the price is higher than the property's income can support under a conventional lending situation.

When the seller is stubborn about his price but not concerned about when he gets it, soft paper can often make the deal workable. If you can pay the asking price, although high, by making the down payment with a soft second, it is possible to come out ahead eventually, provided inflation continues.

Although finding sound real estate is the major task, getting control of it is equally challenging. Property at top price by today's standards may be cheap after a few years' appreciation, but it won't do you any good if you can't gain control right away. Try paying the full price with a low-interest, low-payment second that the income can cover. Be sure to cover your risk by avoiding personal liability. In the event of default, limit the seller to repossession of the property. If you think the property you want shows enough promise to warrant paying top dollar and the seller also thinks it is that valuable, there should be little worry about default. If you are concerned about losing it, maybe you should look for another deal.

ACQUIRE WITH A FIRST AND SECOND—THEN SELL THE FIRST FOR CASH

If you are negotiating the acquisition of free and clear property and the seller wants more cash than you have, here's a method of supplying it.

First mortgages are more easily sold, and sold at less of a discount, than second paper. In this cashless approach, the seller receives two purchase money mortgages: a first mortgage and a second. The purchaser pays no cash.

The purchase agreement is made contingent on locating a buyer for the first mortgage at a price satisfactory to the seller. The sale of the first mortgage therefore occurs concurrently with your acquisition of the property. But it doesn't have to. The seller may get a better price for the mortgage by waiting until it is seasoned. The seller receives the net proceeds from the sale of the first mortgage and keeps the second mortgage. The buyer pays no cash, yet the seller gets the cash he wants.

The purpose of splitting the acquisition between a first and second lien position is to establish a relatively large equity and security position for the buyer of the first mortgage. This will usually reduce the discount necessary to sell the paper.

If the seller doesn't like the idea of discounting the sales price by virtue of the first mortgage sale, you can make up the difference with the second. Just increase the face amount of the second by the amount of the discount. Work in an equal discount amount for an early payoff of the second. Another alternative is to compensate the seller for the discount by adding periodic balloon payments in addition to the regular monthly payments on the second. The point here is to negotiate whatever is necessary to gain control of the property, provided the ultimate profit you make will offset the risk you take.

COLLATERAL SECURITY AGREEMENT

If an owner will not sell without a down payment because he is worried about "getting the property back," this approach may serve to quiet his concerns.

Offer to buy the property with no cash down on a purchase money second. In addition, offer to secure your performance on the second by providing other property you own as collateral.

The equity value of the collateral property should at least equal the amount of the down payment previously requested. You make the deal without cash and the seller gets the security he needs to offset his fears about getting the property back.

The security agreement should be properly drawn by your lawyer and tied to the payment of the mortgage on the property you are acquiring. It should provide for transfer of the collateral to the seller, if you default. It should also provide for release of the additional collateral when the second is paid down to a certain figure. For example, you might include a provision that automatically releases the collateral when the mortgage is reduced by an amount equal to the down payment the seller had originally requested.

Another alternative is to provide for release of the collateral when the acquired property exceeds a certain value as verified by independent appraisal. Calculation of the release provision under this formula is based on the percentage relationship between the new owner's equity and the balance of the loans. When the balance of the mortgage is 75% of the property value, it is, in effect, the same as making a 25% down payment.

BORROW AGAINST YOUR TRUST

If you have money that is tied up in a trust, consider the possibility of borrowing against it. You may not be able to bust the trust and you may not even want to. But if you are fortunate enough to have located sound investment real estate and need to raise acquisition funds, this can be a solid approach.

Bank trust departments often have a difficult time making money on their investments, much less keeping up with inflation or matching the performance of real estate. Taking a hard-nosed look at what the trust department is doing to your money may be a good idea anyway. You may find a move to investment real estate long overdue.

Trusts generally must meet certain liquidity requirements. This makes trust assets excellent collateral. Also there is usually an attempt to balance the portfolio with income-producing assets—normally stocks and bonds that have no aura of risk attached to them.

Consequently, you may have two advantages in borrowing against a trust. You have liquid assets that can usually be converted to cash within a few days and you have income that can be applied toward reducing the money you borrow.

Borrowing against your trust income now to get into sound income-producing and appreciating real estate can greatly improve the overall status of the trust portfolio when you finally do gain full control.

LAND SALE LEASE-BACK

In the final analysis land is the true source of real estate appreciation. Improvements may cost more temporarily, due to inflation, but eventually they will waste away. Insurance companies have recognized the long-term value of land and are actively acquiring well-located commercial income properties. This growing acceptance of the pivotal role of land values in our economic future is the basis for an effective acquisition technique.

With certain types of property you can raise down payment funds by setting up a land sale lease-back. The process involves arranging for a sale of the land under the improvements you're acquiring and leasing it back. The land sale is made prior to your closing, subject to the existing first mortgage, but provides protection for the new land owner by allowing him an out if there's a default on either the mortgage or the land lease. The proceeds from the land sale go to the seller as down payment to cash out his equity.

In essence, you acquire a leasehold interest without cash. You receive direct benefits from rental income and tax shelter for the life of the lease.

Although you are giving up fee ownership with this approach, you may be making a transaction not otherwise possible. There is also the possibility of another benefit here. Depending on the mathematics of the transaction, you may actually be able to sell the land for more than the necessary down payment and pocket the difference. This technique is generally suitable only for larger transactions that have appeal to real estate investment trusts and to other large institutional investors with long-range appreciation in mind.

THE LEASE DOWN PAYMENT

When you are buying from someone who is both owner and tenant of the property, this technique can help offset the down payment.

Consider offering the seller use of the property as down payment. If he plans to keep his business in the same location anyway, you have an opportunity to cover part of the down payment. Essentially, you trade a short-term lease for the down payment.

The seller gets continuing use of his established business location for the term of the lease instead of a cash down payment. You get the property with all its burdens and benefits but without the outlay of cash.

The purpose of this technique is to make a direct move between buyer and seller without the unnecessary step of running cash through the hands of the buyer, then to the seller, and back to the buyer again. Furthermore, if you are able to negotiate a beneficial use for the rent before receiving it, you pick up a time-value advantage that makes the rent worth more when applied in lump sum to the down payment than when it is received monthly.

THE INSTALLMENT DOWN PAYMENT

This technique allows you to acquire property now by paying the seller's equity with installment payments as you raise cash. The income from the acquired property offsets the down payment installments, permitting you to avoid a lump sum cash outlay at closing.

For example, if you negotiate quarterly down payment installments of $3,000 and the cash flow is $500 per month, your net out-of-pocket cost will be only $1,500 per quarter.

The installment payments are secured by placing a purchase money second on the property you are acquiring. As an alternative, consider negotiating an unsecured personal note payable to the seller.

This method can be helpful when you need time to raise a down payment but have competition for the property from other buyers. A pipeline to commercial loan funds won't do you any good if the property is bought out from under you. Tying it down by offering this type of deferred down payment arrangement is far better than missing a good buy. Lenders and other funding sources often can't move quickly enough for you to maintain a competitive stance in fast-moving markets.

ASSUME THE MORTGAGE—SELLER KEEPS THE LAND

This technique permits the seller to retain the long-term benefits of land appreciation while realizing the income benefits of selling the improvements. The seller keeps the land under the improvements instead of receiving a down payment.

There are several ways of structuring this acquisition method that allow you to vary the negotiations to fit the details of the property. As buyer, your primary objective is to acquire the income and tax benefits of ownership by leaving the long-term land benefits to the seller. Retaining land ownership with lease income can be quite an incentive to the seller. Of course, the incentive for you is the acquisition of sheltered income without cash.

Although this is technically a leasehold acquisition, you do assume the existing loans and all the burdens and benefits except land ownership.

One key to negotiating the offer is to split the asking price between the land and improvement values. An imbalance between the two is not desirable. Any difference between the land value and the balance of the existing loans would be paid on a purchase money second.

It is conceivable then that you may end up making three monthly payments: the first mortgage, the purchase money second, and the land lease. Obviously, it is important to make sure that the income is there to meet the payments. After all, this technique is designed to acquire tax-sheltered cash flow. A real danger in any leased land acquisition is the escalation clause, which is generally negotiated by the seller. It is worth a fight to keep any lease payment increase to a minimum.

THE EXECUTIVE INCENTIVE PLAN

If you work for a successful, privately owned company, the solution to your real estate acquisition program may be at the office. Incentive programs have long been recognized as essential to maximum employee performance. This fact of business life combines with the inflation-hedge advantages of real estate to form a technique with solid benefits.

There are several ways to work this cashless acquisition method into a company incentive program. In one case an insurance agency had trouble attracting and keeping good salesmen. In an attempt to provide an incentive that would solve the problem, the owner set up an inter-company real estate sharing program. The company acquired a large office building and arranged for sales staff partial ownership, which increased to a certain percentage based on time with the company. If an employee left without working a reasonable time period, he forfeited ownership in the building. The sales staff grew and made monthly income while building an appreciating net worth because of the foresight of this creative businessman.

Another approach to this acquisition formula is founded on individual employee initiative. If you have a secure relationship with your employer, consider asking to use the company credit line to back up your signature for a down payment loan. Both private and institutional lenders look favorably on loans that are backed by successful corporations. Any loan agreement of this sort should provide for release of the corporation when an appropriate principal reduction is made.

THE HUNDRED PERCENT SOLUTION

One of the most straightforward ways to acquire real estate without cash is to assume the existing first mortgage and execute a second position purchase money mortgage for the entire amount of the seller's equity.

If the seller does not need cash and is satisfied with your track record, a second mortgage secured by his property may be all that is needed to make the deal. This technique is especially designed for sellers who have faith in their property and its future income potential.

A frequent application of this technique occurs when the seller just wants out and is willing to take what equity he has on paper. In this type of situation the purchase money mortgage you offer has more value to the seller than his property. There are more benefits for some sellers in not owning certain property than in owning it, regardless of the potential you may see. This opportunity usually follows depressed markets and is a rare find in high-growth areas.

It is a fact of real estate that you are better off not assuming what a seller will do. If you want a certain property, you owe it to yourself to try to buy it any way you can. Anybody with experience in real estate acquisition will tell you that it is filled with more surprises than you could possibly anticipate—and many of them will be in your favor.

THE PERFORMANCE SECOND

The performance second is used in various applications, including acquisitions with and without cash. It is a downright test of the seller's faith in the value of his property.

With this approach you agree to pay the seller's asking price but make the payments on the second purchase money mortgage contingent on the income of the property. The selling price is calculated based on the return that the seller represents you will realize from the property. In effect, you are asking the seller to share your estimate of risk since you are accepting his estimate of value.

If the cash flow is not there, the seller doesn't get paid on the purchase money second. But if the property performs as the seller represents it will, the payment is made for that month. As an incentive to accept this performance-based payment method, you can negotiate an increase in the payments if the property is more profitable than the seller projects. Setting it up this way allows you and the seller to benefit if he is right. The purpose is to protect yourself from overpriced deals by basing the down payment on the property's performance.

Of course, to measure the income fairly, you must separate operating and capital expense items, so that one-time replacements are amortized over their useful lives, rather than charged in lump sum against a certain month's cash flow. If the seller refuses to cooperate with this approach, you might question the accuracy of the property's performance projections.

BROKER AS LENDER

If you are working with a successful broker, don't overlook the possibility of approaching him as a lending source.

When you consider that he will receive a commission out of the down payment, provided the deal goes through, you can see that he has a real stake in the success of the negotiations. It may be that your broker doesn't have an immediate need for the commission cash but wants to find a high-return investment.

By giving him the opportunity to lend you the cash you need to make the deal, you both benefit. He generates income and places it in a debt investment at the same time. When the alternative is failure because you are short of cash, an aggressive broker will usually lend a helping hand. And for a real estate broker there's no better payoff than saving a transaction that almost slips through his fingers.

THE HIDDEN CO-SIGNER

If you have found solid investment property, you have put the most difficult job behind you. When you reach this point, don't let not having enough money to close stand in your way. There is always a method of getting the job done—you just may not have found it yet.

One of the most easily overlooked ways to bolster that all-important credit line so essential to real estate acquisition is, if you have located the right deal but the bank won't lend you the money to make the down payment, to look for a co-signer. An old friend may be more than interested in helping out. A rich aunt who thinks the world of you may be overjoyed to start you on your way to building a solid estate. All possibilities must be considered when the alternative is losing a unique real estate buy. You may be pleasantly surprised at the help you can find when you strongly believe in what you are doing.

THE INSURANCE POLICY LOAN

If you have built up cash value in a life insurance policy over the years, consider the direct benefits of borrowing against it to buy real estate. Insurance policy loans are one of the cheapest sources of money around. And borrowing against your cash value is like getting your own money back while using it for loan collateral at the same time.

Furthermore, you provide the best additional collateral possible—your own life. And when you think about it, it's hardly a loan—it's really money you have a right to under the qualifying conditions of the insurance policy. Many young couples bought their first house because the husband suddenly realized that the insurance policy a friend sold him in college was like money in the bank.

5

Institutional Financing Methods

If you know the loan variations possible with institutional lenders you can increase your chances of getting the financing you need. Real estate is a credit-dependent industry, and when you know how to work with lenders, you're ahead of the game.

Any loan officer will look favorably on someone who applies for a loan with a sound plan in hand—especially one that will make a profit for his company with little or no risk.

Furthermore, even when what you propose is not within the power of the lender to grant, you establish a starting point for building a plan that is workable. Sometimes a slight change in the way your proposed financing is structured will make the deal.

Easy credit and tight money are the extremes of the lending industry. More than any other business group, lenders are at the mercy of the economics of politics. Government monetary policy will by necessity vary with the national economic cycle in continuing attempts to avoid depressions and to moderate inflation.

From the standpoint of an individual investor who simply wants to operate profitably within the massive unknowns of the marketplace, a few specifics about the lending industry can help. When you know what's possible, you can choose the approach that meets your needs. When you know both what's possible and what meets your needs, you know what to ask for.

New financing methods are being developed continually, especially in the area of government-backed programs. Often the solution to your financing need is to ferret out that hidden government program no one else knows about.

Conventional lending policy varies throughout the country, depending on the local market and the money supply. When you are faced with a lender who is not familiar with what you propose, don't lose faith. No one can be aware of all the possibilities in this fast-moving industry. Furthermore, a technique unfamiliar to your lender is not necessarily an unworkable technique. The best institutional lenders compete for loans and pride themselves on their ability to meet the needs of their customers creatively. New technology in any industry spreads fastest when the profit motive is the driving force. Techniques used in one market can often work equally well in others; just because they haven't yet been introduced doesn't mean they are unworkable. Although lenders want to make loans that are risk-free and profitable, the application that you make for funds must be designed to meet your objectives.

WRAPAROUND MORTGAGE

A wraparound mortgage is an excellent method of obtaining a high loan yield without the usual requirement of lending the full-face amount of the loan in cash. It is a method of refinancing and cashing out the seller without paying off the current loans.

For example, an older center priced at $400,000, with $100,000 down subject to an existing $100,000 first mortgage bearing 7½% interest, is a likely candidate. The new first mortgage is written subject to the existing first mortgage and "wraps around" it. In some areas this financing procedure is referred to as "all-inclusive" and is set up with trust deeds.

You make loan payments to the new lender, who is responsible for making the payments on the existing 7½% first mortgage. The new loan has a face amount of $300,000 bearing 9½% interest, but the new lender is required to provide only $200,000 cash. The additional $100,000 is covered by the first mortgage already on the property. Therefore, the lender collects 9½% interest on the new $200,000 cash and an additional 2% interest on the $100,000 represented by the existing loan—$100,000 in capital the lender did not have to supply.

This approach is a solution to tight money and provides an incentive to the lender with no increase in acquisition costs. The wraparound lender is fully protected. The seller cashes out his position entirely and you are able to finalize the acquisition by establishing financing that might not otherwise be available.

OPEN-END MORTGAGE

Under certain conditions you may borrow back the principal paid on conventional real estate loans. This type of equity loan has grown in popularity as real estate values have increased, but can vary greatly with money market conditions and lender's policies.

The basic approach works like this. If your original loan was $150,000 and over the years it was paid down to $125,000, you have the possibility of reborrowing the $25,000 you've paid and maybe more.

An open-end mortgage allows you to generate nontaxable cash for reinvestment, for further development, or for capital improvements on the property. The lender is able to increase the face amount of the principal and thereby increase the total dollar income from interest. Lenders normally charge fees for this service, which is part of their incentive. But it can be well worth the cost to you if you can make money with the new money you borrow.

SALE BUY-BACK

This technique provides an additional source of profit for lenders and another source of incentive to provide financing. In this approach the developer sells his land to the lending institution and immediately buys it back on paper with release clauses. The developer gets cash from the sale to build, and the lender gets an equity position that increases its profit beyond the restrictions normally imposed by a loan. It also gives the lender maximum security.

This technique allows a developer to arrange financing in a tight money market by providing an incentive to a lending institution through equity participation at the buy-back point. The developer buys the land back on paper and uses the cash from the sale to develop the property.

EQUITY KICKER

An equity kicker can often mean the difference between closing a loan at a reasonable interest rate and not making the loan at all. It provides the lender with a percentage of the income generated by the property in excess of a certain amount.

For example, if the projected base income from a shopping center is $400,000 per year, the loan might stipulate that the lender will receive 15% of everything collected above $400,000. An equity kicker may also call for a percentage of the sale price to go to the lender if the property is sold above a specified price during the first few years of the loan. A skillfully negotiated equity kicker can attract financing in tight markets or with higher-risk projects. It gives that additional incentive often needed to complete a loan: a potentially higher yield.

REO AS INCENTIVE TO FINANCE

Lending institutions that are burdened with REO's ("real estate owned" repossessed property) look more kindly toward making a loan to an investor who concurrently arranges to buy an REO.

You can look on a bank's balance sheet and see the value of the "real estate owned." This property represents an undesirable asset for the lending institution because of the pressure from state banking regulations that limit the time period REO's can be carried on the books.

Repossessed property is a source of available real estate which can often be acquired on favorable terms. It can also serve as a point of negotiation if you're trying to work out a loan. Acquisition of an unwanted REO is contingent on the bank providing the financing you need.

There are many ways banks can help you reach financial objectives. The occasional availability of REO's is another reason it pays to develop a good banking relationship. It's a source of real estate, and with the growing competition for property, all sources for potentially profitable deals should be regularly cultivated.

CERTIFICATE OF DEPOSIT DELIVERY

When a lender is reluctant to refinance property, offer to deposit a portion of the refinance proceeds in the form of a certificate of deposit (time deposit). Redepositing funds from a loan or opening an account with a sizable deposit can often make the difference between getting a loan or not.

Using only part of the proceeds of the refinance to acquire additional real estate is better than not being able to raise the funds at all. Banks and savings and loans need deposits. If you can arrange deposits, chances are that your loan application will get a higher priority than that of someone who can't. The lender benefits by putting a new loan on the books, while concurrently obtaining additional deposits. In times of rapid savings withdrawal, this type of incentive can make a real difference in the decision about who gets a loan.

COLLATERAL ASSIGNMENT

This technique is designed to help when you negotiate a first mortgage and the lender questions either your ability to repay the loan or the adequacy of the real estate you offer as security.

To solve the problem, offer to assign different property as additional security for the loan. The security is encumbered by the bank until the loan is reduced to a certain amount. The process involves a simple pledge of assets by agreement. The collateral may be other real property or personal property. Listed securities are often used.

This technique can help you obtain a loan at a higher loan-to-value ratio. In certain situations it can increase your leverage and significantly improve your return. But, as with all highly financed acquisitions, care must be taken to ensure that the investment will safely produce enough income to pay back the loan and show a profit; the potential reward must justify the obvious risk.

NEGATIVE PLEDGE

A negative pledge is used to protect a bank. It helps you obtain a commercial loan when the bank is relying on the condition of your financial statement at the point in time the decision is made to grant the loan.

The negative pledge differs from a regular pledge by stating that something will not be done. This contrasts with a traditional security pledge agreement which encumbers a specific asset.

A negative pledge states that you will not encumber or dispose of any of the assets listed on your financial statement without written permission of the bank. If you violate the pledge agreement the loan automatically becomes due. The bank is lending money based on your financial statement and the net worth it reflects at the time of the loan. The bank, with a negative pledge, is ensuring that the basis for the loan remains sound. The negative pledge fixes your assets, and if you want to take action that may change your financial position, the bank has a chance to protect the loan. In a way, this is a method for the bank to monitor your finances over the life of the loan.

Pledging to maintain a financial statement in the same condition that it was in at the time the bank agreed to make the loan is a small concession to make if the loan is important to you.

LETTER OF CREDIT

A letter of credit is a useful acquisition tool. Under the right conditions it's as effective as money. It can be used as an earnest money deposit or as a down payment, collectible when and if the transaction closes and the documents are recorded. It is an excellent method of acquiring real estate.

A letter of credit can be used in a variety of situations. For example, it is advantageous when a financially weak but energetic entrepreneur is backed by a financially strong investment partner or group of partners. The backer does not have to come up with cash unless the limiting conditions in the letter of credit are met. A letter of credit is usually exercisable only after a certain date, and only if certain agreed-upon events occur.

When used as earnest money it may, for instance, be exercised only after a commitment for financing is secured. If the limiting conditions of the purchase agreement are not met by a certain date it expires automatically. The key is never to exercise the letter of credit but to gain time with it in order to arrange financing. Attempt to mortgage out before the letter is collectible, or purchase property for resale and turn it over at a profit, without exercising the letter of credit used as earnest money.

For a seller, the letter of credit is solid protection in the event of default on the purchase agreement. When you're acquiring property with it, the letter of credit is an effective method of providing earnest money consideration with someone else's line of credit.

COMPENSATING BALANCES

Many banks will lend money when they are assured of receiving compensating balances equal to the amount lent. This allows a bank to maintain its deposit-loan ratio and, in some cases, may be the only way they can make the loan without depleting reserves. Helping lenders meet the requirements imposed by regulatory agencies and corporate policy is often the only way to get the cash you need.

It is normal practice to lend only to clients who maintain accounts with the bank providing the funds; this is a virtual prerequisite. But if money is tight, it sometimes takes even more know-how to get the loan you need.

A solution that is quite effective involves arranging the deposit of compensating balances by a third party. Your line of credit is therefore offset by compensating balances placed with your bank through an arrangement with another business. Normally the process is worked out with a company who wants your business. Title companies with large amounts of cash in transit can be helpful in this area, when the end result is an increase in real estate closings for them.

ADVANCE PAYMENTS DEPOSIT

You can sometimes convince a lender of your ability to repay a loan by depositing a certain number of the monthly payments at the time the loan funds are disbursed. For example, your agreement might require deposit of the first year's payments at closing and of the second year's payments at the beginning of the second year. You would actually be paying monthly payments in advance annually.

This technique is a way of buying time to establish credit in a new location. It's designed to demonstrate to the bank that although your credit may not yet meet requirements, the source of loan payment funds is clearly established.

The purpose here is to offset weakness in credit history by strengthening the payback method. Keeping in mind that lenders look to credit history and the source of payback funds, combine the two so that the end result will suffice to get you your loan.

HAVE SELLER MOVE HIS ACCOUNT TO YOUR BANK

Since the seller has an interest in the success of your loan, consider ways you can work with him to get the money you need to buy his property. Banks like to make loans when they get additional deposits, and in some cases, they require the checking accounts of the people to whom they lend. The seller may be more than willing to change banks if he knows that is what it will take for you to buy his property.

Will it help get the loan? That, of course, depends on the size of the account and on the competitive stance of your bank. In growing areas, there are usually young banks in real need of new deposits. It can be a pleasure to borrow money when banks are in competition—they can be quite accommodating.

If you're not working with a competitive lender consider moving elsewhere. In any event, if you are able to attract a new (and substantial) customer to your bank as a result of buying real estate with the money you borrow, you have a distinct advantage. The bank benefits on two counts: a new loan to you and a new customer for the bank (the seller).

SAVINGS ACCOUNT TRANSFER

When you are considering the transfer of business to the lender, don't overlook savings of relatives who may want to see you succeed more than they want their current bank or savings and loan association to profit. Transfer of an account can often be done without inconvenience to your helper and it can be timed to prevent the loss of interest.

You may not think a new account is significant, but banking is becoming increasingly competitive and loan officers earn management recognition when they bring in new business. If you help a loan officer build his business, chances are he will be more inclined to help you get your loan approved.

Sizable loans must get loan committee approval. Every committee member you can get on your side will contribute to approval of your loan request, and when you bring a new deposit along with your loan application, that's just one more plus.

BLANKET MORTGAGE

A blanket mortgage is one note and mortgage that encumber two properties. It is used when the primary property borrowed against is not sufficient security for the size of the loan. Release of the additional security is normally provided for when the loan is reduced to an agreed amount and this should be written into the mortgage terms.

One of the requirements for obtaining any real estate loan is the demonstration that there is virtually no risk for the lender. A blanket mortgage is a method of substantially eliminating risk. In many cases it actually oversecures the loan, and that's what makes lenders happy.

With this technique you sign one note and one mortgage that encumber two separate properties. The additional real estate is essentially a method of making up a deficit in equity, and this is the clue to using a blanket mortgage as an acquisition method.

In the best of situations, the property used as added security will, in effect, serve as a down payment (your equity). Consequently, the loan amount may be large enough for you to totally finance the new acquisition. The end result of the procedure is to provide sufficient security for the lender to make your loan. You can accomplish the same thing by selling your additional security property and making a down payment, but that would not be a wise business decision because of the tax consequences and loss of appreciation. A blanket mortgage can be used to meet the lender's security requirements and provide the equity security you need to make the deal.

PARTICIPATION

Participation is syndication of a loan among two or more lending institutions. It spreads the risk and allows small lenders to participate in a loan larger than would have been possible otherwise. It benefits the larger institution in essentially the same way by also reducing its risk.

Generally, two banks or thrift institutions join together to provide funds when one does not have sufficient reserves to undertake the project alone. Their mutual objective, of course, is higher profits at reduced risk.

If the loan you request is too big for your bank, participation with a larger institution may help out. It may take a lender from out-of-town to do the job. Corresponding banks in different cities have relationships designed for mutual benefit. If you live in a smaller town and have a big project, loan participation may be the solution to your problem.

EMPLOYER INFLUENCE

Having real trouble getting the loan? Banks don't like to lose business. Maybe a little pressure from a major depositor, such as your employer, would swing the deal. This can often work smoothly with small banks, especially when competition is rough.

This type of approach is the opposite of providing compensating balances: Instead of bringing business to the lender you arrange for him to keep the business he has. Obviously, banks don't want to lose large accounts and they'll usually do everything possible to make their clients happy. (The exception to this general rule occurs when the bank is poorly managed.) In any event, a little influence from a friend or employer who is a major depositor may provide the incentive for approval of your loan application.

JOINT-VENTURE

Joint-venture development projects are becoming increasingly popular as land and improvement costs escalate. The lender and developer enter into a profit-sharing partnership for the development of a project such as lots in a residential subdivision. Usually the lender or its holding company will contribute some equity in the land and provide some development financing and permanent financing for the home buyers. The developer will also have an equity position in the land and handle all of the lot development engineering and preparation of the subdivision for sale to individual buyers.

Consequently, expertise and financing combine to produce a ready-to-build package for smaller builders. The joint-venture group realizes the profit from lot sales and in the process provides an invaluable service.

Smaller builders are dependent on large companies specializing in packaged land sales. The tremendous increase in raw land costs combined with regulations for open land and environmental protection have forced all but the largest companies out of subdivision development. Joint-venture projects have helped solve this growing problem and worked to keep lot costs within practical limits.

LONG-TERM AMORTIZATION—HALFWAY DUE DATE

This technique is used on older property or in situations where there is concern for the long-range economic stability of the area. The lender is protected by requiring full payment of the loan balance halfway (or sooner) through the amortization schedule.

This may appear to be a burden, but you can cut the amortization term in half by paying an amount equal to the principal due each month, in addition to the regular payment. The net effect is that the loan is paid off before the halfway due date by payments increased each month by the amount of each principal payment. Although the due date approaches quickly, you do have the flexibility and time to get rents up to cover the payments without cutting into cash flow.

This type of loan is designed to accomplish another profit-oriented objective of the lender, which sparks its use with new property. The stated policy is to renew the loan at the halfway due date, but for a fee, and at the rates in force at that time.

Therefore, the lender is not locked into a much lower interest rate established years earlier. It's also an opportunity for the lender to turn over loans more frequently and to increase the net return of each loan investment. It's a more profitable loan for the lender, and along with a strong cash flow, can be a helpful refinance method.

YOU BUY OUR STOCK, WE'LL MAKE YOUR LOAN

A lender with a stock offering that's dying slowly is a lender who needs help. Offer to buy some stock if they will make your loan and thereby free the cash you need to make the stock purchase. But do it informally, so it won't be construed as a loan fee.

Again, this is one more back-scratching method. Help the lender and he'll help you. A loan officer selling stock by direction of management is usually willing to negotiate.

There are many ways to establish solid working relations with your bank. In the last analysis, though, they boil down to getting to know people. If you're serious about acquiring real estate you must develop good banking relations. Stock ownership in the lending institution is definitely an advantage.

STANDBY COMMITMENT

If you have a good project but permanent financing is not available or is too costly, look into the possibility of a standby commitment. It will allow you to get construction financing and build the project, and if you haven't found permanent financing by then, you can exercise the standby commitment and pay off the construction loan. Commitments will often run as long as three years, giving you time to find permanent financing without waiting to build and suffering the added cost of inflation in the meantime.

A standby commitment gives your construction lender the security he needs to make the interim construction loan. It permits you to get the project started without delay. There's another advantage here as well: it's often easier to find permanent financing when the lender can see the project unfold. Regardless, the standby commitment can be a help when money is tight and when the prospects are good that it will be more readily available later.

THREE YEARS WITH A BALLOON

If you are buying property that you plan to sell within three years, this technique can increase your yield. Structure the loan for the down payment so that monthly payments are low, and there is a balloon at the time you are ready to sell. Then pay off the down payment loan with the profit from the sale.

When you structure this approach correctly, the return can be very high. You are able to borrow the entire amount of the down payment and then pay it off from the sale proceeds that flow from future appreciation. The property actually buys itself. The cash flow and ultimate resale proceeds are the down payment. You simply set up the transaction so that the down payment is paid out of the profit rather than out of your pocket.

LESS THAN FIVE YEARS SECURED

Commercial banks don't like to lend money for more than five years, and for a loan of that length they normally want security. Knowing this in advance can help you structure your deal to meet their requirements and plan for the cash flow you need to make the deal work. The most beneficial approach is to structure the transaction so the cash flow from the property will pay off the down payment loan in five years. If you can negotiate a purchase with this in mind and then take a workable proposal to the bank, you have a head start on getting the loan.

Much of the success you have with banks depends on your loan presentation. When you're trying to borrow equity money (the down payment) thoroughness and accuracy go a long way toward soothing a loan officer's anxiety about risk. When the lender can see clearly that you know what you're doing, the level of risk associated with the loan drops drastically. Approach borrowing to acquire real estate the same way you would approach borrowing for a business.

Commercial banks specialize in business loans. If you go in for a down payment loan with an income and expense history of the property and a projection of its future performance, a real estate loan begins to look more like a business loan, and that is what banks feel more comfortable with. Set up your loan request as thoroughly and accurately as you would for a business loan. Look at your personal financial statement as a company balance sheet. Structure the property history like a business profit and loss statement with a projection for the future. The more business-like your loan request, the more likely the response will be positive.

EIGHTEEN MONTHS UNSECURED

If you plan to borrow on a personal note with no amortization, apply for less than an eighteen-month term. This is generally the limit banks like to go on signature loans. If your signature is security enough and the short-term due date is manageable for you, this type of loan is a good source for down payment funds.

If you apply for the loan with a specific payback plan in mind, it will be that much easier for the loan officer to approve the loan. There are two essential requirements which lenders must see in your loan request. First, there must be adequate security. Within certain limits your signature may be security enough if you are well established in the community. Second, there must be a source of funds to repay the loan. Optimally, the income from the property will meet this requirement; your salary can help also.

THE BRIDGE LOAN

If you're moving out of town and don't want to wait to sell your old house before buying a new one, this might be the answer.

Before you leave, arrange a short-term loan with a local bank for a portion of the equity in your house and secure it with a second mortgage. The due date should be set far enough ahead to provide time to sell your old house, but should also be due if the sale occurs earlier. Another approach is to borrow the down payment from a bank in the town to which you are moving, with the understanding that it will be paid when your old house sells.

This is one application of a very helpful financing technique. When there is a time lag between two events and your funds depend on their concurrent completion, a bridge loan is a practical solution. The proceeds actually bridge the two points in time.

For example, if the seller must close within thirty days but your financing is not available for ninety days, there is a sixty-day time gap that must be covered to save the deal. A bridge loan may be the way to do it.

FINANCE COMPANY SECOND

Finance companies are an increasingly popular source of loan money. They recognize the value of lending on homes that have experienced a high degree of appreciation and are willing to lend money on the difference between your first mortgage and 80% of the appraised value. This permits you to borrow back a portion of the first mortgage you've paid, plus a percentage of the appreciated value of your house. The interest rates are high, but you can generally stretch the payout over ten years. If the funds are wisely invested, the loan can be worth the cost.

Although your home is solid enough security for the finance company, due consideration should be given to certain aspects of the transaction. Will the profit from the investment of the loan proceeds pay the loan back, cover the interest costs, and yield a high enough return to justify the risk involved?

Care should also be taken that you don't take a deep step into debt just prior to a major economic contraction. It's when the good times look like they'll never end that you want to be careful, especially with your home. Consider also that capital debt must always produce a solid investment return and never be used for consumer purchases.

COMMITMENT LETTER

If you must close an acquisition now but the mortgage rates are high and show signs of dropping soon, a commitment letter may help you. First, get a letter of commitment from a savings and loan association agreeing to lend the money you need at today's rates. Then, go to a commercial bank and use the commitment letter as security to borrow the money to close. When the bank loan is due (six to nine months later, usually), the rates for permanent financing may be lower. But if they're not, you can exercise the commitment and live with the higher interest.

The alternative is to let the commitment letter expire and to apply for a loan at a lower rate. When a change in rates gets underway, the movement is rapid, regardless of the direction of the trend. Usually the turnaround points are reasonably identifiable and the trends in interest rate changes are obvious. If a change in trend indicates a lower interest cost a few months down the road, purchasing a commitment letter and setting up a short-term loan may be well worth the trouble.

6

Techniques For Negotiating The Most Advantageous Private Financing

One look at the variety of methods for negotiating the acquisition of real estate is enough to light fire in the heart of any serious entrepreneur. It's also a fair test for anyone who questions the strength of his interest. There are probably as many people scared by unstructured opportunity as there are people turned on by it.

People who are attracted by the virtually unlimited potential of real estate tend to do exceptionally well as they learn more of what can be done. Each new technique forms the basis for another chance to replace someone else's problem with an opportunity-creating solution.

Ultimately it's your application of the vast and growing body of real estate methods that will measure your success and there's no better area for applying this solution-oriented approach than in negotiating the details of a privately financed acquisition.

A privately arranged acquisition that is not restricted by the mysterious reasoning of institutions or government sponsorship can take shape like a symphony. Today's techniques are the starting point for what you can do. The more you know the more you can do to expand the opportunity before you. And when you are negotiating with flexible, knowledgeable people there's really no limit to what you can accomplish.

BUILDER'S BAILOUT

Builders and developers who have an inventory of unsold homes are able to take advantage of this often-used technique. It helps the builder out of a tight spot and can help you acquire a home without a large down payment.

You actually bail the builder out of his construction loan. This is done by making a small down payment and having the builder carry back a portion of the difference between the sale price and the first mortgage. For example, a $50,000 home is more easily sold to someone who can buy it with a minimum down payment. Under normal market conditions, the down payment is approximately 20% of $50,000 ($10,000). But as a sales promotion for unsold inventory, the builder may be more than willing to sell with $1,000 down to qualified buyers. You arrange for a first mortgage of $40,000 and the builder carries back on a second mortgage for $9,000.

This technique gives the builder an aggressive sales plan for buyers who have high incomes, but not a large amount of cash. It allows a qualified buyer to purchase a home and receive the immediate benefits of ownership on terms that are quite an incentive. Builders have been saved from bankruptcy with this approach. It provides them with relief from the interest burden of carrying the construction loan and protects their profit with the second mortgage.

OVERPAY

Overpaying the asking price is a negotiation technique designed to secure benefits that are more valuable than the price. Applying this technique requires judgment and timing during negotiations. You certainly don't want to pay more if it's not necessary. You only want to offer more if it's the only way the seller will accept your offer.

In consideration for paying more than the seller is asking, you may negotiate easier payout terms, a lower interest rate, or a smaller down payment. It can also be used as a lever to obtain releases for certain portions of the real estate being acquired.

This technique is designed to provide an incentive for the seller to concede on terms that he might not otherwise consider—terms which are more important to you than the price of the real estate. If you can't meet your profit objectives without acquiring the real estate, this technique will ensure that you get the property. The seller can be rapidly motivated when he realizes more of a total profit from the sale of his real estate than he had originally anticipated or even requested.

CONTINGENT PRICE SALE

A contingent price sale is an acquisition at a value to be determined by the future performance of the property. The sales price is set as a function of the income production of the property.

This technique is often used in the sale of a business and can make the difference between a successful acquisition or a failure when you suspect hidden problems. There are a number of ways to structure the payout details with this approach. Generally, though, you should capitalize the operating income over a given time period to establish the total sales price. Although the seller may require a minimum base, you can establish the maximum total price by dividing the annual income by the return you want. For example, an average annual operating income of $50,000, divided by a 10% return, results in a price of $500,000. If the income is $45,000, the sales price drops to $450,000 if you want a 10% return. This is just one of many ways to structure a contingent price sale. A variation in the price formula may be necessary to account for the effect of the financing.

Another application is to avoid a base sales price, and simply agree to pay the seller a specified percentage of the profits over a limited time period. If you are involved in a contingent price sale, be sure to investigate the tax advantages to the seller. The general benefit is that gains from sales do not have to be reported until the sales price is final. With proper tax counsel the seller may find the tax advantage worth the risk of a contingent price.

PRIVATE WRAPAROUND

One of the most beneficial ways for a seller to carry the balance of his equity is a wraparound mortgage. This can be structured by using a number of different instruments such as a mortgage, trust deed, or real estate contract. The particular document used can best be determined by your state law; the financial benefits will be the same.

The procedure is simple. The seller receives a first lien position subject to the existing loan, which is paid monthly out of the buyer's payments on the new wraparound. The seller gets interest on the dollar balance of his equity, plus additional interest on the difference between the existing loan rate and the higher interest on the wraparound.

This is an excellent method for a seller and can offer an incentive for other concessions when you are negotiating an acquisition. If the existing loan is $80,000 at 8% interest, and the seller agrees to a wraparound mortgage at 9½%, here's how it would work. With a sales price of $160,000 and a $20,000 cash down payment the seller's equity balance is $60,000. But the face value of the wraparound mortgage is $140,000. Consequently, the seller receives interest of 9½% on his equity of $60,000 and 1½% on the underlying 8% mortgage of $80,000. This can be quite an incentive for a seller who knows how to calculate the long-term benefits of compound interest.

SELLER AS SHORT-TERM LENDER

This is a method of working with the seller to avoid high interest rates. If the seller wants terms that require refinancing, but interest rates are too high for you, this approach may solve the problem.

Negotiate with the seller to carry the amount that would have been paid off by refinancing. Then set a due date a couple of years away at the maximum, or sooner if you obtain a satisfactory loan rate.

This will allow you to close the transaction now and give you the chance to set up permanent financing at a lower cost as interest rates drop.

VARY THE LOAN PAYMENTS BASED ON OCCUPANCY

This technique ties the payments on your purchase money mortgage directly to the occupancy of the property you acquire.

For example, if you're acquiring a 20-unit apartment complex with a questionable future, structure the financing with the seller so that if the occupancy rate is 90%, the interest rate on the carry-back loan stays at 9%. But if occupancy drops to 80% the interest rate drops to 8%. The reduction would continue at a ratio of a 1% drop in interest for each 10% drop in occupancy.

There are a couple of variations to this approach that can be helpful. If occupancy drops below a certain rate you might want a temporary suspension in amortization of loan principal and pay only the interest until things improve. Another variation is to decrease the total amount of the loan payment rather than just the interest. In some cases where the loans provide for a large monthly amortization of principal it may not be necessary to decrease the amount of interest paid at all. The object is to decrease monthly debt service to avoid a negative cash flow. Whether you can lower the interest or principal portion of the payment depends on what the seller can live with.

IMPROVEMENT COSTS AS RETURN OF DOWN PAYMENT

If you are acquiring property that is really run-down and a questionable investment due to its present condition, consider putting the cash that would normally go to the down payment into repairs. You can protect your position and the seller by setting up the purchase to upgrade the property.

It's not unusual for property to be sold because the owner is unable or unwilling to spend the money necessary to bring it up to its market potential. Furthermore, it may be necessary to put a certain amount of money into the property just to protect it. By agreeing with the seller to divert the down payment to repairs, you will give him better protection on the equity he carries on a purchase money mortgage. It's certainly better than the alternative.

Consequently you are able to acquire real estate in a condition that ensures a profitable operation. The seller, of course, gets his full purchase price in the form of the purchase money mortgage, and you get your cash outlay (that would have gone to the seller) back in property value.

Putting the down payment into improvements may be necessary to ensure both a profitable operation and the timely payment of the seller's carry-back mortgage, but there's another benefit as well. If the seller insists on cash there's a possibility he may get more in the long run if the improvements are sufficient to permit refinancing. This would of course cash out the seller and may increase his willingness to take the deal.

MORATORIUM ON DEBT SERVICE

If you are acquiring a one-tenant building and there is a question as to whether the lease will be renewed, some degree of protection can be insured by negotiating a halt to loan payments if the building becomes vacant. Usually you will have to put a limit on the time of the moratorium, with the understanding that the purpose is to give you enough breathing room to find a new tenant. Three to six months is a valid starting point.

By including this relatively minor provision in a purchase money mortgage, you may avoid a serious problem in the future. The objective is to lessen the risk of acquiring income property that depends on the continued occupancy of one tenant. A warehouse acquisition is a likely candidate for this type of protection.

AUTOMATIC DISCOUNT

An automatic discount should always be part of your acquisition strategy. When you're acquiring property with a substantial purchase money mortgage and there's a possibility of refinancing it in the future, this technique can mean real savings.

For example, a $100,000 carry-back mortgage on a $150,000 purchase might provide for an automatic discount of 10% (about $10,000) if fully paid within two years. The objective of the seller is to provide an incentive for the buyer to cash him out. Consequently, a drop in the discount after two years to 5% is an appropriate extension of the technique. Of course, when you're acquiring the property and paying on the note, you will want the longest time possible at the maximum discount the seller will accept.

This technique allows you to reduce the total sales price by transferring the bargaining point from the property to the note and mortgage. For many sellers the possibility of a future cash-out is solid incentive to reduce a sales price, and negotiating it into the future gives you breathing room to get the job done. Even if it is impossible to work out, you lose nothing by setting the possibility. There's always the chance you will resell the property to a cash buyer during the discount period, and then the importance of the discount will be measurable as money in your pocket.

INTEREST ONLY UNTIL THE FIRST IS PAID

By negotiating an interest-only payment to the seller until the existing first mortgage is paid, you can minimize the drain on cash flow from debt service. This technique is especially helpful when the seller is asking a high price and you want to maximize the tax shelter aspects of the property.

There are, therefore, two major benefits to this technique: an increase in your cash flow, because you are not paying off the principal balance of the purchase money mortgage, and a more efficient use of the available tax deductions, because the interest payment is fully deductible.

This technique is a sound way of maximizing your profit in any situation, but in some cases it is essential to the profitability of the acquisition. You are, in effect, asking the seller to defer payment of the equity represented by the purchase money mortgage. From a time-value standpoint, money in your pocket today is more valuable than money to be received in the future.

When the cash flow is questionable, this approach helps offset the risk. It's one more aid that can be combined with other techniques to minimize risk and maximize profit.

BALLOON PAYMENTS

Structuring private financing with well-timed balloon payments can often mean the difference between completing a transaction and letting it die from lack of ingenuity. A balloon payment is a lump sum principal payment that comes at the maturity of a note. But balloon payments can be placed at various points throughout a loan to provide an incentive for the seller to accept a smaller down payment or some other terms you may want.

One clever application is the Christmas season balloon, which calls for an additional lump sum payment each year during the first part of December. The strategy here is to give the seller a Christmas incentive to offset other terms of the acquisition that are important to you.

Periodic balloon payments in addition to the regular amortization payments can often lower the amount of down payment required by the seller. Knowing that he will receive beneficially-timed balloon payments can be more important than a single large down payment. The beginning of April is another date to keep in mind because of income taxes.

The other benefit from balloon payments is that they can be used to structure an installment sale. Rather than lose the important benefits of installment reporting it is much wiser to spread a down payment over a couple of years in the form of a balloon payment.

When you are acquiring real estate, balloon payments can help defer an immediate cash outlay for the down payment. But the way you time the payments will provide the incentive for the seller.

SELL WITH OPTION TO BUY-BACK

If you're having difficulty getting a seller to part with his property, offer him an option to buy it back. This can be a solid form of protection for someone who thinks he may be selling too soon, and it's a small concession for you to make when the alternative is no transaction at all.

The terms of the buy-back option can be very flexible. You should build in a reasonable profit in case the seller does exercise the option. The danger in this technique is that the seller has a marketable right in the option and may choose to sell the option, itself, to someone who wants to exercise it. To prevent this, you can negotiate a clause that makes the option non-transferable.

This approach has been used successfully in joint ventures with options to buy partial ownership. In one case an investor retained an option to acquire a 25% ownership position in an office building developed on his land. The option had a five-year life and was eventually sold for a substantial profit when an insurance company bought the entire project.

There are several ways this technique can be worked into the specific requirements of any transaction. It aids property acquisition when the seller wants to have his cake and eat it too. But it's also a financing tool for a seller who wants to raise money by selling now, while still retaining the possibility of buying his property back later.

REDUCE THE INTEREST BUT INCREASE THE CONSTANT

When you are negotiating private financing, the major objective is to retain as many benefits as possible, whether you are buying or selling. One way of structuring an agreement to get the benefits you want is to vary the components of the constant annual amortizing percentage that is applied to the loan balance. A portion of the constant percentage is applied to interest and the remainder reduces the loan balance. For example, a loan with a 9½% interest rate, which amortizes over thirty years with equal monthly payments, has a constant of 10.10%. This percentage represents 9½% interest and .6% loan reduction.

This technique uses the constant to satisfy the seller's desire for rapid payoff. Instead of putting a due date toward the end of the loan, you reduce the interest and increase amount of constant (the total loan payment). The net effect is an increase in the speed with which the seller receives his total sales price.

It will also increase the amount of loan payment that he can allocate to lower capital gains tax rates. When you use this technique, you benefit by paying less interest, and therefore, less total dollars (interest plus principal) over the life of the mortgage. Of course, you will have a slightly smaller interest deduction, which may be of no consequence depending on other shelter aspects of the transaction.

REDUCE THE CONSTANT BUT INCREASE THE INTEREST

Another method of using debt service payments to your advantage is to reduce the constant but increase the interest. If the seller wants long-term income, increase the interest rate and maintain a low portion of the loan payment for principal reduction. This will stretch out the term of the loan payoff and give the seller a large dollar amount of ordinary income from interest. It will also increase the total cost of the property acquisition, but your current net tax deduction will be larger due to the increased interest-to-debt ratio.

The point here is to meet the seller's requirements without destroying the profitability of the property. This approach allows the seller to maintain the size of his capital (loan principal) and receive income from it as interest over a longer period of time. As a trade-off for stretching out the amortization, the cash flow of the property is increased as a result of smaller debt service payment.

SALE LEASE-BACK

A sale lease-back is one of the most effective real estate acquisition methods. It is frequently used by large businesses but it can be equally beneficial for any size transaction when the seller is both financially sound and wants to continue using the property.

This technique builds income into the transaction. Essentially, the seller agrees to sell and lease-back at a rental rate based on the sales value of the property. This establishes a rate of return without the usual concern about finding tenants.

A sale lease-back is often used when an owner wishes to raise cash without losing use of the real estate. The objective is to obtain capital for the business to finance expansion. If a corporation is in a sound growth industry, why tie up capital by owning real estate? The business will make more money by concentrating on its specialty rather than by owning real estate. Consequently the sale lease-back can often be viewed as a financing method from the seller's point of view.

Acquiring property that is leased back by the seller can give you quite an advantage. With a financially strong seller signing the lease, it's possible to obtain 100% financing. Of course, the details of sales price, interest rates, and lease terms play an important role in the profit you are able to structure.

ADD THE INTEREST TO PRINCIPAL

A property which does not have adequate cash flow to cover the debt service of a second mortgage allows you the opportunity to pay interest only, with no amortization of the second mortgage principal. When experiencing extreme cash flow problems, part of the interest not covered by income can be added to the loan principal. This is one temporary solution to the negative cash flow created by overfinancing or by inadequate rental income.

This is a limited time measure designed to give you an opportunity to increase the income on the property. Not all property starts out making money, and if you're acquiring property that won't cover the debt service required by the second mortgage, this technique is a way to buy time.

And really that's what you do. As the interest increases, the loan principal compounds rapidly, raising the amount of indebtedness on the property. But in some cases it takes only a little time to turn property around. This technique allows you to negotiate a loan that is designed to satisfy both the seller's requirements and the limitations of the existing cash flow on the property. It provides time to set up a turnaround program that will make the property productive.

The object is to build the income up enough to amortize the loan principal with interest. Although this is a somewhat undesirable position to be in, there are benefits. The seller gets the added compounding value of interest paid on interest. It increases the total dollar return he will get for the property and compensates him for the delay.

THREE-YEAR INTEREST-ONLY BALLOON

A three-year interest-only payment followed by a balloon for the total amount of the mortgage can be a helpful way to structure the acquisition of vacant land. If you anticipate a resale within the three-year period, your return will be higher if you can minimize amortization of the debt.

The objective here is to resell the property prior to the balloon. The funds for payment of the balloon come from the new buyer's financing. In the event that the property is not sold, you have ample time to locate financing to pay the balloon as it becomes due. This is a logical opportunity to build in a request for a discount if you make the balloon payment early. It's a natural for an automatic discount.

The all-cash payoff at the end of three years is the incentive for the seller to accept interest only. It may hit that middle ground between all-cash at closing and a long payout that meets your needs and the seller's.

SUBORDINATION TO CONSTRUCTION FINANCING

If you are ready to build but don't have the cash necessary to pay off the existing loan, subordination is one solution. The holder of the existing financing simply agrees to subordinate his security position to a new construction loan. When building is complete and permanent financing is established, the existing loan is paid in full. Consequently, there is a period of increased risk for the existing note holder, because if there is a default, the construction lender will have first claim to the property.

Also, if you're planning to acquire vacant land for development and want to maximize leverage, negotiate subordination of the seller's interest to construction financing as part of the purchase. This will allow you to build without paying off the land until construction is complete and the permanent financing is in force. This approach works to maximum benefit when combined with a mortgage-out strategy.

SUBORDINATION FOR CASH

If you own property that can be refinanced, ask the holder of the first mortgage to subordinate his mortgage to a new first mortgage. As an incentive, you might agree to pay an extra amount on your existing loan. With that unexpected cash incentive, the first mortgage holder may be willing to accept a secondary position, thus giving you the opportunity to pull out tax-free cash for acquisition of more real estate.

Subordination of a first lien position is normally associated with development, but it can also be a successful method of raising cash for acquisition. Vacant land that is encumbered and ready for development is the usual candidate for a subordination agreement, but it can be equally as effective when you want to raise acquisition capital, whether your property is improved or vacant land. The only requirement is that it can be refinanced. The problem, though, is convincing the note holder to take a subordinate lien position. It is an increase in risk.

Therefore, to offset the increase in risk an additional cash payment is made. Ideally this payment will reduce the existing loan. In difficult situations, though, it may be necessary (and profitable) to pay an added cash bonus over and above the loan amount. It can be well worth paying a little extra when the end result is tax-free cash in your pocket. And, if the economics of the property support the new loan safely, the note holder will be in a better financial position than before.

7

More Private Financing Techniques

One of the most rewarding aspects of acquiring real estate is saving a transaction that almost fails. Anyone who has been associated with real estate no doubt has seen a fair share of earnest negotiations end in disappointment. And it's twice as frustrating when both sides want the deal to succeed but can't seem to find the pieces necessary to complete the puzzle.

It's the desire for a mutual end without the means to reach it that brings private financing methods into effective use. These techniques are paths that reduce negotiations to a routine of choosing the best of several alternatives.

Each new method you discover through your own efforts should be saved for future reference. Every combination of documentation and financing should be jotted down. One of them may be just the formula that pushes a valuable transaction over the last barrier. Real estate problems exist only because the appropriate solutions have not yet been found. The more techniques you have in hand, the greater your chances of turning someone else's problem into your opportunity.

Acquiring real estate requires persistence. And the people who seem to have the knack for it are people who never seem to give up. They ignore people who say "you can't do it." They keep trying to structure deals long after others have given up.

Furthermore, these athletes of the real estate business seem to have a built-in ability to shut out the boos of the spectators—

the ones who criticize while they watch but can't muster the wherewithal to play the game. The doers either force the creation of a workable transaction or move on to the next opportunity, with little concern for the difficulty others perceive.

More likely than not, the end product of this ongoing process is a series of transactions sculptured from old, time-tested techniques modified by that individual touch of creativity that comes from a positive can-do attitude.

The flexibility of private negotiation works well for anyone willing to enter the field with a solution-oriented view of business. These are the techniques that provide the best selection. But look at them as only a starting base for the new methods you will discover as a result of your own efforts.

PURCHASE MONEY MORTGAGE

This popular approach is often used when the seller wants installment reporting and/or when institutional financing is not available. The seller deeds to the buyer, and the buyer gives a note secured by a mortgage to the seller. The seller consequently has a first mortgage position secured by the property he has sold. In the event of default, the seller forecloses. This is a private adaptation of standard institutional financing without the transfer of lump sum financing. The seller gets his money as the payments are made.

It is really a form of documentation, as are many of these techniques. Often both buyer and seller know where they want to end up and the only requirement is setting up the paper work to get there. That's one reason why it's important to know these techniques; then you can explore alternatives with the seller during negotiation. It's the exploration process that can touch on new alternatives entirely acceptable to the seller. How many real estate transactions do you suppose have failed simply because the people involved didn't have access to the alternative that would get the job done? How many fail because when the solution appears, they accept someone's offhanded remark of "impossible" or "that won't work"?

REAL ESTATE CONTRACT

Sometimes called a sales contract, land sales contract, or contract of sale, this approach to private financing provides a practical solution to the problem of foreclosure. The buyer literally contracts with the seller to purchase real estate. The real estate contract and the deed-conveying title to the buyer are held in escrow until the terms of the contract are met, then the deed is recorded. A special deed is also placed in escrow deeding the property from the buyer back to the seller. This deed is recorded only if the buyer defaults under the terms of the contract and eliminates the lengthy foreclosure process; it's final, there is no redemption.

Real estate contracts are usually set up as standard printed forms in states where they are commonly used. The terms and details of the document vary in different localities depending on state law.

The benefit of the real estate contract is the flexibility it provides for the buyer and seller to establish terms which meet their mutual objectives. It can be especially useful when you assume the existing mortgage and the seller accepts a down payment that doesn't cash out his equity. The real estate contract makes up the difference. Its face value is the seller's remaining equity. When the contract is paid, usually by monthly payments, the escrow agent (often a bank) releases the deed, and the property is yours.

SECOND MORTGAGE OR SECOND TRUST DEED

When a buyer assumes an existing loan the seller will often be forced by reason to carry back a portion of his equity on a second mortgage or trust deed. In this approach to private financing you get a deed to the property subject to the existing loan.

Rather than sign a contract that must be performed, you sign a promissory note secured by a second mortgage.

In some states a trust deed is used instead of a mortgage. There are legal differences from state to state, but for our purpose the important factor is the negotiation possibilities of the documentation.

One element that any buyer should pay close attention to is the extent of personal liability in the event of default. As real estate prices rocket above reasonable measures of value, there are certain considerations that should be kept in mind when signing notes for real estate acquisition.

In the event the bottom drops out of the economy and you lose your real estate, what happens under the terms of the note and mortgage you sign? If you paid more for the property when you acquired it than its worth under the depressed market conditions in force when you lost it, there can be a negative consequence. If it can't be sold for enough to pay off the notes you signed, the mortgage holder can sue you for the deficiency—the difference between the market price and the amount you owe. If the court rules against you, a deficiency judgment is handed down which requires you to pay up. If you don't, your other personal assets can be attached and sold. This is one good reason not to allow yourself to get caught up in excessive speculation—you can lose more than the property itself.

Any good real estate financing technique can be used imprudently, but don't let it happen to you. If you are acquiring property that has even the remotest possibility of ending up in trouble, insist on a limit to personal liability on the notes you sign.

PLEDGE, COLLATERALIZE, OR HYPOTHECATE

Using additional collateral is often a help in closing an acquisition, especially when the down payment is less than the seller feels is necessary for security against default. Insurance cash value, stocks, bonds, personal property, or other real estate all serve the purpose.

If the seller feels he needs a 20% down payment but you have only 10%, take a close look at other assets you own. Determine what the seller is trying to accomplish by requiring a 20% down payment. If he just wants security and can wait for the cash, hypothecating anything of value can provide it.

The key here is finding out what the seller wants. That's why it can be crucial for someone involved in negotiations to know thoroughly what the seller wants to accomplish and what he really needs to accomplish it. It may very well be that his primary objective is to get out of management headaches, and that a no-down-payment sale to an effective manager would be more satisfactory than 20% down by someone who will ruin the property and default on the mortgage.

PRIVATE INSURANCE ANNUITY

An income for life can often be more appealing to a seller than a sale. One solid way to provide income is to purchase an annuity from an insurance company that will continue for the life of the seller. The seller deeds the real estate to you free and clear and receives an income for life. The property is refinanced to generate the cash necessary to buy the annuity.

Another approach to acquisition by annuity is used among relatives. It has greater flexibility and does not involve the outright purchase of an annuity. An annuity agreement is used that establishes payment terms. It simply states that payment for life will be provided as consideration for the property.

In this case the seller relies only on the private agreement for future income. That, of course, is why it's generally more appropriate for use with relatives. Certainly there's no reason why this unfunded approach could not be used by unrelated individuals if there is sufficient trust between them.

The obvious benefit here is having free and clear income-producing property that you don't have to borrow against to purchase the annuity. It can serve as the basis for building a solid investment portfolio and can provide the income to pay the annuity.

PURCHASE A REMAINDER INTEREST

In some situations the only way a seller will part with his property is if he can retain use of it for the rest of his life. You can accomplish this by purchasing a remainder interest in the property and by allowing the seller to retain a life estate interest. The seller gets all income from the property until death, in addition to the cash and notes you pay at closing.

This technique may be combined with a management agreement permitting you to operate the property to protect your interests. Upon the death of the seller, the entire fee interest automatically transfers to you.

Purchasing a remainder interest illustrates how a transaction can be closed even when the timing is not exactly right. It's a solution for what may seem to be an insurmountable barrier. It is also potentially very beneficial for the seller; the cash from a sale now may be much more useful than it would be after death.

Since you're not receiving income during the balance of the seller's life, there is a certain price adjustment that can be made to compensate. This may be offset, though, by the property-appreciation factor, which may be necessary in calculating the remainder interest.

WALK THE MORTGAGE

This technique has many applications. Walking the mortgage is a process of substituting different real estate as security for an existing mortgage. The mortgage is modified or rewritten so as to encumber different real estate. The objective is to free property that can be easily refinanced. It is a technique that can provide significant future benefits if you negotiate it into the terms of property you're acquiring. Even if it isn't agreed to in advance by the seller, it's an excellent method of maximizing refinance proceeds if you can negotiate it later.

The significant factor is the flexibility that walking the mortgage gives you. When you arrange to take a mortgage off, you free equity. Equity is acquisition power. This technique really hits home when you use it to refinance appreciated property.

In one case, an investor was able to walk a $45,000 mortgage from a four-plex to a large tract of vacant land. Although the land was solid security, banks wouldn't lend on it. But the individual who held the purchase money mortgage on the four-plex was happy to cooperate—especially when he received a $1000 incentive.

REVERSING THE INTEREST

By structuring an acquisition with separate notes that are due annually, you can place the high-interest payments at the end of the amortization term rather than at the beginning. Negotiate the transaction so that each note is paid, plus accrued interest, at the end of every twelve months. For example, the first note will bear one year's interest, the fifth five years' interest, and the twentieth twenty years' interest. Each year has a separate note. It may take twenty years of $10,000 notes to pay off the property. One mortgage is used to secure all the notes.

This technique intentionally places the burden of large payments on the later years. It also gives you a larger deduction toward the end of the amortization term. The seller is able to defer ordinary income in the earlier years of the sale because the interest is reversed. This approach can be of benefit to someone who is retiring and anticipates being in a lower tax bracket as time passes. Consequently, it would be advantageous to take a greater portion of capital gains now and defer receipt of the higher-taxed interest income. However, be careful with this one. Compound interest grows quickly.

THIS YEAR'S INTEREST AS DOWN PAYMENT

The use of several years' prepaid interest as down payment has been eliminated as a beneficial tax technique available to purchasers. This advanced deduction was a help with taxes, but it can still be used to some degree as a negotiating advantage when you are purchasing property at the beginning of the tax year.

If you are buying with virtually all paper and little cash, offer to pay the balance of the year's interest in advance, in lieu of a cash down payment. This may give the seller the cash necessary to put his mind at ease. It will also increase his effective yield on the carry-back paper. When used in conjunction with an interest-only mortgage, it results in an acquisition with fully deductible dollars.

The most advantageous acquisition methods are those that do not require use of your own cash. When you can't quite reach this ideal objective, the next best approach is to maximize the deductibility of the cash you do put into the acquisition.

Often, a down payment requirement is half need and half greed. If you can negotiate out the greed part and make the balance tax-deductible interest, you'll take a big step toward maximizing your profit.

THE BARGAIN SALE

The bargain sale is a method of structuring complete deductibility and minimum taxable income during the initial years of ownership. In this approach the seller agrees to reduce the sale price of the property in exchange for the entire net income for a specified period of time. The time period during which the seller retains income is based on the amount of price reduction. The price reduction is more than offset by the continuation of rental income flowing to the seller.

The seller or a third party manages the property, giving the seller a chance to earn more than was taken off the asking price.

It is the potential of unspecified income that makes this technique pay off for the seller. The main advantages for the buyer are a large deduction and appreciation, in anticipation of capital gain on resale.

When you acquire using a bargain sale structure, immediate tax advantages are established. You make no equity down payment. Any cash paid to the seller at closing is structured as interest paid on the acquisition note to the seller. You receive no net income. The portion of the rent you do get is limited to the net operating expenses. Consequently, you acquire the property at a bargain price and set up a maximum tax-deduction deal. The property depreciation and price reduction return as second-wave benefits when you sell at reduced capital gains rates in the future.

Furthermore, the deal is intentionally structured so the seller has a very good chance of receiving more for the property than under a conventional sale. The keys to the seller's added profit are management ability and the rental market potential during the time period he has the right to income.

Solid profit incentive is built into the transaction for everyone. This technique demonstrates as well as any that with cooperation and creative effort, maximum benefits can be structured for both sides, ensuring a winning situation for buyer and seller.

DIAMONDS PLEDGE OR CUTTING THE DOWN PAYMENT IN HALF

Diamonds of investment quality can be expected to appreciate an average of 17% per year. If you can find the right partner for your real estate deal, they can be bought wholesale.

Instead of paying cash as a down payment, buy diamonds wholesale and use them to secure a note for the down payment in an amount equal to the retail value of the diamonds. Then pay off the down payment note using the income from the property.

The diamonds used as note security are purchased at wholesale price—half of the retail value and half the amount required for a down payment. The other advantage of this technique is that the diamonds will be appreciating at a rate practically twice that of the interest on the note. If you negotiate an interest-only note with a due date in five years, the diamonds will have doubled in value and could be sold to pay the note. Using this application, your down payment is fully covered by diamond appreciation.

This is a high-leverage technique that gives you the advantage of double-asset appreciation. Your cash, which would normally go to the seller as the property down payment, is put to double use. It buys security for the down payment note (the diamonds remain your property unless you default) and the appreciation is yours. Then the note acquires the real estate, which also appreciates at a high rate. When you consider that your cash is depreciating with inflation, putting it to use to acquire appreciating assets becomes even more profitable.

LOWER THE INTEREST AND INCREASE THE PRICE

This method decreases the ordinary interest income to the seller, but makes up the difference in capital gain from the sale. The seller's after-tax income is increased through the benefits of capital gains without causing him to sacrifice the total cash in his pocket.

If you don't mind losing an interest deduction, this technique can have an impact on your success when there's competition for property. The first effect is that it gets the seller's attention by offering more for the property. The second effect is that it demonstrates how the low interest-high price adjustment will convert a large portion of the combined sales proceeds (interest and principal) to lower capital gains rates. The net after-tax dollars will be greater for the seller, but the same for you.

The key to this technique is to calculate the total dollars you would pay for the property at a certain high-interest rate. Then calculate the total at a much lower rate. Add the difference to the seller's price. He pays a lower capital gains rate and gets more net after-tax income, even though the total dollars he receives is the same.

Although you lose an interest deduction, it may be a small price to pay when competition for property is rough and the alternative is failure in closing the deal.

REDUCE THE PRICE AND PAY POINTS

If you prefer to increase the deductible portion of the transaction and the seller is carrying a note and mortgage, this technique can help.

Offer to reduce the sales price and offset the reduction by paying points. You will be able to write off the amount of the loan points over a short period of time (a down payment, of course, is not deductible). If the seller will accept the ordinary income from the points, this method will reduce your after-tax costs for the property.

This technique neither increases nor decreases the total dollars received or paid. It simply converts part of the total to a deduction for you. If you negotiate with this technique at the seller's asking price, it is possible that the reduction in price will be what he was willing to accept anyway, and the points, in that case, will be icing on the cake.

MANAGEMENT FEE FOR SPECIFIC SERVICES

If the seller is to be involved in the management of the property after the sale, this technique can help reduce your net cost. Structure part of the offer as payment for management services.

This approach is another way of building a deductible payment into the acquisition. Management fees for specific services per-

approaches designed to ease the tax problems of parting with investment or business property.

In many situations a tax-free exchange is the only sound business approach for a real estate owner. The procedure is simple and safe when you know the IRS rules. Essentially, you sign an exchange agreement with the seller stipulating that you will purchase real estate he designates and then make the exchange. Normally, a time limit for finding satisfactory property is arranged. Until the exchange is completed or the exchange agreement expires, you are protected—the owner cannot sell to someone else. When suitable exchange property is found, you sign an agreement to purchase it, contingent on the terms of the existing exchange agreement. Then you proceed through closing.

Exchanging involves a little extra tax knowledge and paperwork, but is well worth it when the alternative is failure to make a profitable acquisition.

ACQUIRING PROPERTY FROM A REAL ESTATE CORPORATION

Public corporations are required by the financial community to demonstrate earnings-growth performance. This is practically impossible for a real estate corporation to do under accepted accounting standards. The problem is that depreciation lowers reportable profits. Although a public real estate corporation may have solid cash flow, property depreciation write-off tends to lower reported earnings for financial statement purposes. Consequently, the company appears to be in bad condition when it may be in excellent shape. That is, earnings are lowered on paper but not in fact. It's a conceptual gap in standard accounting practice.

This technique is designed to help the corporation generate earnings while providing investment property for you. Approach the real estate company with an offer to buy 75% of a given property. Require the company to guarantee a 9% cash return on your investment before depreciation. If cash flow is generated above your guarantee, the company receives a 9% return on its 25% ownership interest. Any additional cash flow is split 50/50, not 75/25. You get a solid 9% return. The company generates capital for expansion and is able to report the gain from your acquisition as annual earnings. Furthermore, 75% of the depreciation is elimated from the balance sheet, while 50% of the growth in cash flow is retained. (This technique is particularly suitable for shopping centers that have high-income growth.)

Often the solution to acquiring real estate is mathematical. Although it may appear that nothing worth buying is for sale, a closer look at the needs of property owners can change their problems into your opportunity.

8

Methods Of Using Leases To Acquire And Finance Real Estate

Land may be the backbone of real estate, but leasing is the muscle. Real estate starts with land and becomes a business with a lease. Land is a store of value. Leasing is a method of extracting the stored value.

It's the use of real estate that produces income. By definition, when you're working with the leasing process you're involved in the use of real estate for the production of income. From an investment standpoint, it is often the nature of the lease that establishes both your profit potential and the management demands placed on your time.

Shopping centers have become sought-after investments largely due to the accepted practice of tying a lease to the gross sales of the tenant. A percentage lease ensures the center owner growing income as the tenant's business prospers. Often the tenant succeeds only because of the drawing power of the shopping center and profits far more than is possible in a more isolated location.

Triple-net or absolute-net leases have demonstrated investment benefits of a different kind. If you're after management-free ownership they're the answer. Often used with the sale lease-back of single-use buildings, they provide reasonable returns without the problems of management.

Leasing can also play an important role in your acquisition plans. It ties directly to financing as proof of income to service debt. In fact, when you look for acquisition financing and have a solid lease in hand, you're practically in business.

BOND LEASE

One of the most reliable, often-used ways to acquire real estate with a minimum of cash starts with the bond lease. This technique requires a tenant with a high credit rating who is willing to sign a long-term lease. The best candidates are national corporations with "A" ratings.

The basic process involves using the lease to secure your financing. Whether you're building a new building or buying an existing one, the commitment to lease is the first step. The lease is security for the financing and, in effect, it guarantees repayment of the loan.

Usually, the lender requires that the term of the lease equal or exceed the time required to amortize the loan. This approach can also be used with smaller individual companies showing good local credit ratings.

Using a bond lease to acquire real estate has an obvious and immediate benefit: you start with a reliable tenant. This fact opens the door to financing, and when you have both good income and financing, you're well on the way to a profitable transaction. The key is to put all the components together so the net result is a positive cash flow for you.

LEASE-CONDO

This technique is designed to give potential tenants incentive to buy professional office space that is difficult to lease. It can form the basis for acquiring property no one else can deal with; the decision to buy real estate is easier when you see a way to make a profit that others have overlooked.

Offer current tenants and prospective new tenants space for a certain period of time: four years for instance. In your proposal agree to apply part of the lease payment as credit toward purchase of the space leased. Structure the lease so the tenant will have accumulated enough credit toward the down payment to make the purchase without additional cost.

This is an incentive for the tenant to set up business in a building that may not be in the most desirable location. It is a solution, also, for an owner who is having difficulty leasing. It is certainly better than having a building, which can't be sold as an investment, sit vacant.

There are certain important requirements that must be worked into the project. Conversion to condominium space has become widespread and is a common practice in many areas, so the mechanics are somewhat routine. Since you're dividing the ownership, you will need to have the individual spaces surveyed in order to establish legal descriptions. Of course, individual financing will be necessary for each professional office.

SANDWICH LEASE

A sandwich lease is an excellent method of controlling property and generating investment income without capital. The key is leasing property that can be released at a higher rate. Your lease is then sandwiched between the owner and the new tenant, who pays a higher rent to you than you pay to the property owner.

You can use a number of methods to get the initial lease at a lower rate. If the market is depressed, maybe the owner would be happy to lease it at a rent lower than you calculate the market will be after the slump turns to a recovery. If the property needs work, agree to upgrade it if the owner will give you a long-term lease at a low rate.

Negotiating economically is the key here, but including an

option to purchase as part of the lease is also important, especially if you turn the property around.

By signing your lease when the general market is depressed and by putting personal effort into upgrading the property, you may realize a drastic increase in its value when rental conditions improve. Furthermore, when you release at a higher rate, the property value will automatically increase based on an income approach to appraisal. Its investment attractiveness will improve overnight, and with an option to purchase at the previous value, the profit will be yours.

MASTER LEASE AS SECURITY FOR DEVELOPMENT

A master lease is an overriding lease of a building (usually an office or shopping complex). It is used to guarantee a return to the owner in a sale lease-back transaction, and in some cases, to secure permanent financing. The developer of a project may underwrite its sale to a limited partnership and concurrently provide security for the long-term lender by establishing a master lease. The signatory to the master lease then covers his obligation by leasing to individual tenants at a profit.

In a way the master lease is an insurance policy against loss of rent. Its purpose is to establish a base return on investment for the owner and in some cases a guarantee for payment of debt service during the rent-up phase of a new development.

When you acquire property with a strong master lease signed either by someone who knows what he is doing or a company with strong management and financial capabilities, it reduces your risk. It also increases your ability to obtain equity financing. Be careful, though. If the property itself is headed for trouble you may be forced to depend on the party signing the master lease. Of course, this is the purpose of the master lease, but when things don't work out as planned, even the strongest companies may try to renegotiate or cancel.

MANAGEMENT LEASE-BACK

This approach is often used when selling apartments to a limited partnership. A management company, which is more than likely a subsidiary of the company selling the limited partnership units, will lease the entire property after the sale. The limited partnership, therefore, has no concern over management, and the sales organization has a built-in aid. By arranging the lease-back concurrently with the offering, the investors know what their return will be and will be more willing to invest.

This is an application of the master lease designed to meet the needs of investors who must be satisfied with both the professional management and projected return before committing their funds. It brings the risk down to a minimal level.

Real estate companies that specialize in limited partnership offerings are expected to provide management for the property they sell. Often they have a separate corporation staffed by professional managers who handle this. A management lease-back actually transfers economic risk from the investors to the management company. The company is compensated for this risk by the income produced in excess of the lease-back obligation.

Consequently, negotiation of the master lease must take the normal management fee and the risk premium into consideration. The end result is more income for the company and less risk for the investors.

LEASE BACK THE VACANCIES

If you are acquiring property that has a high vacancy rate, ask the owner to lease the vacant units for a certain period of time to ensure your return. The seller only has to lease enough units to bring the cash flow up to a reasonable return. This approach avoids the extensive liability of a master lease-back and provides a method of reducing the seller's obligation as the vacant units are rented to new tenants.

Leasing back the vacancies is one of the many ways of working around apparent problems to structure a successful closing. If you are acquiring property with vacancies that make the real estate risky financially, this technique may help.

Sellers who are tired of managing and are willing to work with you are often able to share risk to ensure a sale. If the transaction is on the borderline between problems and profit and you need that little incentive to go ahead, offsetting the vacancies can turn a questionable deal into a positive venture.

LEASE CASH-OUT

If you are acquiring land that has potential for a lease, locate a tenant at the same time you make the purchase. Then take the lease to a lender as security, in addition to the land itself, and borrow the money to acquire the land. Income from the lease will offset the loan payments, and the land seller will cash out, possibly at a price favorable to you.

This is a technique that converts a potentially passive land investment into a business opportunity. Any time you can change the earnings performance of property concurrently with acquisition, you tend to increase value. When you enter an acquisition that involves making raw land income-producing, you move considerably closer to a business proposition.

Arranging a lease for the land you want to buy is like creating the money you need to make the purchase. The future income represented by the lease has a present value. If that present value equals your purchase price, chances are you can acquire the land without cash.

The seller's cooperation will be essential; he has good reason to help out. When you finish putting the pieces together, the seller will cash out. As you proceed be sure to make the steps interdependent. Make the purchase contingent on financing and finalizing a land lease. Offer to cash out the seller only if every part of the transaction fits together as planned.

LAND SALE LEASE-BACK FOR DEVELOPMENT

By selling and leasing back commercial land, you can often raise the cash necessary to complete development. Construction costs sometimes exceed the funds available for building. Consequently, a developer may have to sell part or all of the project land to raise development funds.

You may be able to raise sufficient cash by selling the parking area to an investor and leasing back. The land investor's interest would be subject to construction and permanent financing. You are able to add cash to cover construction and complete the project.

Selling property and leasing it back is a common financing technique. Applying this method to parking areas and free-standing portions of a shopping center, such as automobile repair centers, simplifies the requirements you must follow. In fact, if you anticipate the possibility of needing additional funds, try to hold back these somewhat separate land areas from your construction mortgage. This will keep you from having to negotiate a partial release if you have to structure a land sale lease-back later.

PACKAGE THE LEASES AND SELL OUT

This approach is designed to give you a rapid turnover of capital by packaging the entire project (including leases, financing, land, plans, and the construction contract). Virtually all of this is done on paper, with a minimum of out-of-pocket expenses. The cash comes when the package is sold to an investor at a profit. The cash outlay by the investor covers the real estate equity requirement and the equity you create by putting the package together. The investor gets a fully organized project and none of the headaches of putting it together. This approach is often used for establishing limited partnerships.

It takes skill and hard work to set up a successful shopping center or office building development. Getting solid tenants signed to leases is as valuable as land ownership is over the long pull. The value created by the leases is saleable. Selling a complete project package is a way of pulling out the value created by your efforts. It's a quick turnover of the capital invested to put the deal together without the wait normally associated with long-term real estate investment.

With the steady growth in federal requirements and bureaucratic regulations, the value (and of course the cost) of packaging a sound development project is increasing. As a business segment of the real estate industry, it has solid potential.

LEASE WHEN YOU CAN'T BUY

If you have spent time trying to acquire land, no doubt you have run into owners who refuse to sell but will lease. Although it is frustrating, the wisdom of their plan is apparent. Even in this situation there are advantages.

Leasing land eliminates the need for large amounts of front-end capital. Furthermore, if you plan to build and the land owner agrees to subordinate his interest to the financing you need, the possibility that you will be able to mortgage out is greatly increased. You will be able to put the deal together with less cash since you don't have to buy the land. By leasing land you gain control. What you do with that control will determine your profit. In that sense, it's no different from outright ownership.

The extent of your long-term success with a land lease will depend largely on what you are able to include or to exclude from the original lease terms. Try to work in an option to buy. Work toward an option that can be exercised after a reasonable time period, but push to get one in even if it's exercisable in fifty years or only after the death of the owner's last child.

It's crucial to avoid imprudent and short-sighted rent escalation clauses. Don't tie increases in rent to the consumer price index; it has been proven to be very dangerous. If you have to include a provision for rent increases, and it would be unusual if you could avoid one, tie it to the long-term appreciation of the land and not to the sporadic annual jumps in value that tend to be nothing but an appraiser's best guess. Keep in mind that you're renting the land, not offsetting the owner's loss in buying power due to inflation—his continued ownership of the land will do that, not your rental payments.

LENDER LAND LEASE

This approach to financing often provides the incentive a lender needs to fund a project. The lender buys the land intended for development and leases it to the developer. Since the lender will be providing the first mortgage, the fear of subordination that is common with leasing landowners is absent. The lender (usually an insurance company) has full security, and the developer gets capital for the land acquisition from the lender, in addition to long-term financing, thus reducing the need for equity capital.

This technique is a joint-venture approach to a sale lease-back that eliminates the intervening step of acquiring the land. Instead, you line up your lender and go into the project completely funded. The lender is really your backer and is investing in your ability to create a business out of vacant land.

From the standpoint of long-term investment, the lender has an advantageous position through the ownership of appreciating land that also produces current lease income. From your standpoint, the strategy is to package the project, to mortgage out, and to generate sheltered income.

LEASED LAND PYRAMID

Buying land subject to improvements and existing financing and then leasing it back to the seller is an increasingly popular investment method. It is as good for small investors as it is for insurance companies. You can use leased land as a rapid estate-building tool by simply varying the capitalization rate.

For example, if you buy a land for $10,000 and lease it back to the seller based on a capitalization rate of 10%, your rental income is $1,000 per year. At this point, you own the land and receive lease income on it. Then exchange the land tax-free based on a 5% capitalization rate. The $1,000 per year income has a value of $20,000 when capitalized at 5% ($1,000 ÷ 5% = $20,000). You double the value to $20,000 and increase your acquisition power overnight. It's a matter of negotiation, but also, of risk evaluation.

This technique illustrates how you can build value into a general acquisition plan. There's a lot of truth to the statement that you make your money when you buy.

SALE LEASE-BACK AS AN INVESTMENT OPPORTUNITY

The sale and lease-back of successful business real estate is an excellent source of investment real estate. Under the right conditions you can use this technique to bring property on the market.

Corporations often prefer to put their capital into expansion rather than having it tied up in real estate which sustains current operations only. Every dollar of capital applied to the business serves to increase earnings, and having equity tied up in real estate can in some cases actually slow down corporate growth. In the more fortunate situations, earnings will grow as fast as capital permits the company to expand. Approaching companies unaware of this opportunity is one way to locate investment property when there doesn't seem to be anything worthwhile on the market. Due to the competition for investment real estate, techniques which provide an incentive for the seller can be invaluable.

The sale lease-back has a history of financing business expansion. From the standpoint of the company it is an investment capital-generating technique. Traditionally, the larger national corporations have put it to effective use, but it works equally well with established and growing small businesses.

SELL AT A LOSS AND LEASE THE LAND

You can sometimes develop an opportunity by taking a look at the components of a particular real estate investment. For example, if the value of the improvements has dropped but the value of the land has increased, consider structuring the acquisition so that the seller has a loss on the improvements but retains ownership of the land. There are solid benefits for both sides with this technique.

When you purchase improved real estate, set up a depreciation schedule that requires allocation of value between land and improvements. It is not uncommon for the land to appreciate and the improvements to depreciate during a given ownership period. The degree to which this occurs depends on the position of the property in the real estate cycle and on general market conditions.

If the property you want has the right characteristics, here's a benefit you can offer the seller that may provide the needed incentive to close the deal. If the improvements are worth less than the seller's adjusted basis, buy them separately and lease the land. The seller will have a deductible loss on the sale and will lease income from the land.

Work in an option to purchase the land after a certain date. You'll eventually get the land if you want it, and in the meantime, you'll be able to allocate the entire purchase price to depreciable improvements while deducting the lease payments.

USING A LEASE TO GAIN POSSESSION BEFORE CLOSING

Leasing has many applications that go beyond the conventional association with space rental. It is a fundamental real estate tool that can help build a solid acquisition structure in various situations.

For example, if mortgage rates are killing the deal you're working on, consider escrowing the down payment and leasing the property until the money market eases. The seller will have a firm deal, with cash in escrow to back it up, plus lease income. You get use of the property now and time to arrange for more satisfactory financing.

Leasing the property you want is a method of bridging a time gap that market conditions often present. (The gap can be years long when you lease with an option to buy.) Uncomplicated textbook investments are the exception in actual real estate practice. The time when you want possession is not necessarily the time when requirements of the transaction will permit possession. For instance, the extended time demands of a multi party exchange often include a lengthy period of searching for suitable property that will complete the transaction. If you want possession of the property as soon as possible but the owner must exchange for tax purposes, the delay can be prolonged while the search for exchange property is underway. There is a solution, though.

In addition to the standard exchange agreement, which will probably provide for several months necessary to locate exchange property, arrange a separate lease so you can gain immediate possession. The rent should be based on fair market rates and run for a certain period with provisions to renew. It will allow you to have use of the property and yet to cooperate with the seller's objective of securing the tax benefits of an exchange.

9

How To Use Options To Acquire Real Estate

Options hold a special place in real estate acquisition. They are rights to purchase without the obligation to perform associated with a conventional purchase agreement. In some highly leveraged cases an option increases in value at a much greater percentage rate than would be possible with an outright purchase of the underlying property. An option also carries an implicit time advantage.

In fact, when you buy an option you really buy the time you need to choose an action. If you choose not to acquire the property under option, it will expire at the agreed time with no consequence other than the forfeiture of its cost (if any), without benefit realized by you.

The time you buy with an option can be put to many and varied uses. It's standard operating procedure to obtain a few months option on land to run soil tests and check out the title and municipal requirements before making an all-out commitment to commercial development.

Options are also a useful speculation method. If you see progress moving toward an overlooked parcel of land, a well-negotiated option can put you in the position to profit. It's timing your commitment that will make the difference. If you move too soon and the buyers haven't reached you before the option expires, you end up out-of-the-money. Of course, who's going to wait? If you're really out to profit by reselling the option, you'll probably know the likely buyer even before you commit. In any event, options can take many forms and are adaptable to a number of different circumstances.

The basic option structure includes the price and terms for purchase of the property, the date, the right to transfer the option, and a provision allowing for extension of the option. Variations on this structure center around how the owner is compensated for granting the option, including the amount and timing of payment. These negotiable terms can have a direct effect on your profit if you plan to resell the property or to develop it. Obtain the option you need; that should not be a problem if you're serious about buying and willing to pay a fair price.

Whether option costs should properly apply toward purchase, or rest as separate payment for the time the property is off the market, is negotiable. In fact, it depends on which side of the table you're sitting on. Certainly, you want to negotiate the best deal possible for you.

INTEREST OPTION

An interest option is an easy method of paying for an option. Although it is not quite as good for the seller as other option structures, it is a sound way to calculate option value.

With this approach, the option consideration is an amount equal to the savings account interest on the value of the property for the period of the option. The details vary with circumstances. In some cases the seller is paid only if the option is not exercised; if the option is exercised, the seller gets his price but no option consideration. Consequently, the option payment is compensation for loss of the sale and is made after the expiration date. If the option is exercised and the sale closes, there's no penalty to the seller (and no option payment) because he reached his ultimate objective: selling the property.

It makes sense to tie an option payment to the property value even if the interest rate is a negotiable item. The owner may prefer that the rate be tied to the prime lending rate or the consumer price index; there's considerable flexibility on this. For example, it may make sense to the owner that you also agree to pay the property taxes prorated over the option period. Although it may be a minor amount for a few months option in light of the total sales price, it can appeal to a seller.

EFFORT OPTION

Option structures are as flexible as the people negotiating them. Look at what you want to accomplish and you'll very likely find a suitable option method. An effort option stipulates that you will obtain preliminary development plans and all necessary municipal approval within the option period, at your expense. If you don't exercise the option, the plans, engineering studies, and other documentation, including any lease commitments you've obtained, become the property of the seller.

Since the value of land is mostly determined by its use, this approach shifts a degree of uncertainty toward the seller by allowing you to verify the property's suitability, with no cost for the time needed to do it. If the property proves to be unsuitable for development, all you've lost is the cost of investigation. The seller is not paid for the cost of discovering that his property is unsuitable for your plans.

Turning over the results of your effort is simply a way to negotiate option control. The paper work done on a certain parcel has value even if it merely eliminates a piece of property. This option approach reduces your costs and it covers a portion of the risk when there's a chance that a particular location is not practical for your project.

LETTER-OF-CREDIT OPTION

A letter of credit can eliminate the need for cash while meeting the seller's requirement for option security. With this technique you give the seller a letter of credit in the amount of the option consideration mutually agreed upon. If the option is not exercised, the seller collects on the letter of credit; if it is exercised, the letter of credit becomes null and void.

The seller is fully protected in the event you don't complete the acquisition. And you avoid the initial out-of-pocket cost of a standard option. With this approach there is no additional payment to the seller above the property cost. The letter of credit is primarily a guarantee that you are earnest in your plan to complete the purchase.

The cost to you, assuming the purchase is complete as planned, will probably be no more than the interest charged by the bank for issuing the letter of credit. From a negotiation standpoint, though, you gain the same advantage you would by paying cash when the option is signed.

AN AUTOMATIC ROLLING OPTION WITH FIRST RIGHT OF REFUSAL

This technique illustrates how an option can be combined with other provisions of an acquisition to meet your specific project goals.

An automatic option occurs when exercising one option automatically establishes another option to acquire adjacent land. The owner grants subsequent options as you exercise the prior ones. When exercising your initial option, you automatically roll it over to adjacent land without an additional payment.

The consideration for each option is built into the purchase of the previous parcel. It may not be necessary that the purchase price be increased in order to obtain the option. The cash from your initial purchase and the probability of additional sales can be enough incentive to satisfy the owner.

An added benefit to this approach is that although your legal option rolls only from one parcel to another at a time, there is a built-in first right-of-refusal to the entire tract which may include dozens of separate parcels. In effect, you tie up an entire project with only the expense of acquiring the parcels you need, when you need them.

CONTINUING OPTION

A continuing option is set up by assigning income from paper, which you own, to the owner of the property you are optioning. The property owner receives monthly income for a designated period, after which the option expires if not exercised.

This approach avoids a large up-front payment and depending on the terms can provide the extended time necessary to sell the option for profit. It should be set up for a limited time with the right to renew for another period equal to the first.

The purpose is to build in continuity. First you establish an ongoing right by monthly option payments from the income-producing paper assigned to the property owner. The more he gets used to regular income, the less likely he will be ready to give it up. Second, you build in the right to renew or extend the option for a term equal to the original period. By providing for a continuing option, you build in profit potential when your objective is to speculate on the value of the property over an extended time period.

INCREASE PAYMENT OPTION

This technique is designed to increase the option consideration in return for annual renewal. The initial agreement provides for increasing the payments to the seller if you choose to keep the option in force.

This is an incentive for the seller to grant a long-term option and allows you to tie up future appreciation early in the game. For example, you can structure the payments so the seller receives $1,000 the first year, $2,000 the second, and $3,000 the third year, but $5,000 the fourth year and $8,000 the fifth. The longer you control the property, the greater the payments made to the seller.

It may also be appropriate to increase the purchase price as the option period progresses. If this requirement becomes part of the deal you may be able to offset it by applying part or all of the option payments to the purchase price. This can become a necessity toward the end of the option as payments increase faster.

LAND COST OPTION

Option consideration can be an excellent method for a seller to offset the costs of holding vacant land. With the right approach to negotiation, you can secure a relatively long-term option by simply paying the taxes on the property. If the owner knows he has this expense covered, and maybe a few other costs, negotiation of a long-term option can be smoother.

One of the drawbacks to investment in land that doesn't produce income is the cost of holding the property over a long time period. Unfortunately, many land buyers don't discover this until they experience it firsthand.

A property owner who has been hit with this realization is a likely candidate for the negotiation of an option that will lower his costs. It's the unexpected that hurts the worst; a new paving or municipal utility assessment has brought more than one parcel of land on the open market. If you size and time the option payment to cover the owner's costs, chances are you'll get his attention and have a good foundation for acquiring the property.

REAL ESTATE AS OPTION CONSIDERATION

Deeding free and clear real estate or partial ownership shares can often be an effective option technique. By using the value of the land you have, you can acquire an option on additional real estate.

One of the best applications of this technique permits you to transfer value from lots far from developing areas to property that is rapidly appreciating. The objective is to meet the basic requirement of sellers when granting options—to get a little extra consideration for giving you the right to purchase.

For example, a subdivision of mountain area lots that never got the public attention necessary for success can be a source of solid option consideration. Offering an owner one lot for a year's option to buy property you believe will appreciate, can allow you to cash out of the mountain lots. Your option cost is essentially equal to the value of the lot. If you time it right, you'll be able to sell the option for more than the cost of the lot and make a profit.

10

Techniques For Building Value And Protecting Your Real Estate

For many, every investment action is ultimately directed toward building value and protecting what is owned. In a sense this is the objective you may have in mind when applying the methods in this book. There are techniques, though, which specifically seem to satisfy these purposes. They include ways to create value by dividing property into smaller units, improving flexibility and increasing your profit. There are also techniques that are directed toward creating opportunity—methods you can use to start an effective acquisition program. Finally, there are methods you can use to protect yourself and to solve problems that inevitably accompany a long-term association with real estate.

USE SWEAT EQUITY TO INCREASE VALUE

One time-tested way to start building a portfolio of real estate holdings is to fix up the property yourself. Making it a hobby or family project can be financially and emotionally rewarding, if you don't mind taking the time to learn how to do the work efficiently.

ACQUISITION FROM THE TRUST DEPARTMENT

If you are in a long-range program of acquisition, you no doubt know that the major problem is finding property that meets your investment criteria. Certainly, the type of financing terms you are able to negotiate will to a large degree increase the beneficial value of the property. Since the search is so difficult, it helps to know that some of the best sources of investment real estate are the trust departments of your local banks.

Generally, the management of real estate is a problem for banks. They are seldom geared toward real estate management, and consequently, prefer to advise their clients to make more passive investments. Trust officers often know property owners who want to sell. Establishing a rapport with the bank officers in your area can lead to a number of investment opportunities.

THE PARENT-CHILD ALLOCATION

The parent-child allocation is a technique that establishes a 50/50 ownership but allocates the tax benefits based on the economic strength of the parent and child. In the initial years of ownership, the debt service is allocated so that the parent pays the interest portion of the monthly payment and the child pays the principal.

Therefore, the larger burden of the debt service in the early years (interest) is borne by the parent, who more than likely needs the accompanying tax deduction. In the later years of ownership, the child assumes an increasingly large share of the debt service as the interest portion of the annual constant decreases.

The important point, of course, is that the parent receives the majority of tax benefits in the early years of ownership and rightly so, since the parent's financial strength realistically places the liability and greater economic burden of ownership on him or her. The partnership balance is then equalized in the future as the interest portion of the debt service declines and the principal payment increases.

USING AN INSTALLMENT SALE BETWEEN RELATED PARTIES

Generation-skipping techniques have to a large degree been limited by tax laws. There is, however, a method that can provide some help in this area. It involves a sale of the parents' real estate to their children with no money down on an unsecured personal note. The note is then paid out of the property income.

Since the property is not used as security for the note it may be refinanced, thereby providing funds for additional real estate acquisition. The parents, then, will the note to their grandchildren. The property may be exchanged for larger property if that proves advantageous in the future. This is a method of combining the major remaining devices of protecting real estate equity from tax—the installment sale, refinancing, and the nontaxable exchange.

SUBDIVIDE BEFORE PURCHASE

This technique is based on the principle that smaller portions command higher prices. If you are acquiring property that can be easily divided, consider doing it concurrently with acquisition, so that at closing you have two parcels instead of one.

This builds in future value and increases flexibility when you are ready to sell or exchange. The property must be divided by legal description, and the financing must be separated so that no overlap restricts the subsequent sale.

SPLITTING THE FEE INTERESTS

You can often increase the profit of a real estate investment by viewing the various fee interests as separate values. Are the water rights saleable without reducing the value of the surface rights? How about the mineral rights? Could you lease a 50% interest to an oil company that would like to protect its future exploration area? What about leasehold interests? Could you lease the land now and actually increase the value to an investor? And what about the gravel deposits? Is there a concrete company that might be interested in buying the sand and gravel and then restoring the surface? Real estate is more than land; even air rights are sold and leased in densely populated areas. When you are ready to sell or exchange, look at the entire bundle of rights that constitute "real estate."

DIVIDE THE DEBT AND REFINANCE

If there is a problem with the marketability of property because of the size of the debt, consider dividing it into smaller loans secured by portions of the property, or by different property. Property that is overfinanced can be made marketable by carving off a portion of the loan or removing a second mortgage, and placing it on a different property acceptable to the lender (maybe a first position on a free-and-clear house). This approach can also create equity for exchange.

DIVIDE THE OWNERSHIP BASED ON CONTRIBUTION

Cash is not necessarily the most crucial element in real estate acquisition; the more you know about financing, the less important it becomes. If you are putting a project together, consider apportioning the ownership based on the contribution of the partners to completion of the project, rather than on their bank accounts. Anybody can have money, but not everyone can put together a successful real estate project.

One partner may have a background in land development and cash, so he puts up cash for 25% and effort for 25%. Another partner may have cash but no experience and, therefore, puts up cash for 25%. The third partner may be putting the financing, land acquisition, and leases together, and has no cash, but earns 25% of the ownership. The cash involved meets the equity requirement, but the ownership is divided based on the skill value contributed by each partner, value that is essential for the project's success.

RESORT CONDO

Motels and hotels in seasonal areas often have a difficult time making consistent profits, so they are frequently for sale. By establishing a legal description for each room and setting up the financing correctly, you can sell the motel as a condominium. Return customers are likely buyers, and the seller can retain management for a fee. Each new owner gets rental income when not using the property, and the former owner gets management income, sale proceeds, and in extreme cases, safety from foreclosure.

MEDICAL CENTER OFFICE-CONDO

Older medical centers can present a problem when they are out of vogue and the doctors move to newer space. The problem exists because the property does not offer sufficient benefits to draw tenants. By dividing the complex into individual office units and leasing them with an option to buy, or by selling them outright, you can solve the problem.

Also, changing the image of the complex from a medical to general professional office can increase the size of the market for tenants. Consequently, by selling offices to the user, you can often turn a complex around and increase its market value by increasing its value to the market.

This approach can be used with certain apartments as well. In fact, converting apartments to condominiums has become so widespread that the procedure is simple routine and is readily accepted by many financing sources.

MOVE THE HOUSE AND DOUBLE THE BENEFITS

Older houses located on land needed by expanding companies can be the start of a money-making opportunity. Buy the property along with a vacant lot that is appropriate for older residential housing. Move the house from the more valuable land to the other lot, fit it up, and rent it. Then lease the newly cleared lot to the institution.

This will create greater equity in two properties because you've put each to more appropriate use. Negotiation during acquisition must be done with the plan in mind so that the financing accommodates the ultimate objective. Value is increased when property is put to its most productive use.

USING PAPER PARTNERSHIPS

Investment clubs among business friends are quite common, but they usually apply their collective efforts toward fighting the stock market. The argument against group investment real estate centers around the demands of management, but qualified real estate management companies are readily available.

Even so, if real estate is too much for your club and you're tired of the stock market, consider acquiring discounted paper secured by real estate. Essentially, this is the same investment medium of our most conservative institutions: savings and loan associations. With the right discount, you can often borrow all the money necessary to acquire the paper. Borrowing to buy at a discount and using the income from the paper to repay the loan can form a powerful method of pyramiding without cash. When you undertake the project as a group, you can greatly strengthen your borrowing power and accelerate your investment success.

BUY PAPER AT A DISCOUNT AND TRADE AT FACE

One of the best estate-building techniques is buying paper at a discount and, with careful negotiation, using it as the down payment to acquire real estate. With this technique, you can pick up immediate profits while moving from a declining debt investment (paper) to an appreciating equity investment (real estate). But expect to pay tax on the profit if you convey ownership of the paper.

ASSIGN THE PAYMENTS—DON'T TRADE THE PAPER

Rather than conveying ownership of the paper as down payment, establish an escrow agreement that assigns the payments from the paper to the seller as security for a new note with identical terms. The seller receives the income from the paper as consideration for the down payment. You still report the income from the paper on your tax return, but you spread tax on the profit over years, as it is received, when this approach is structured correctly.

LOWER THE DEBT BY INCREASING THE INTEREST

Market value of property is sometimes lower than the loan balances as a result of vandalism, fire, or overfinancing. The key element in solving this type of problem is having low interest on the original loans. If you start with low interest, you can negotiate an increase in the interest rate without increasing the total monthly payment, and concurrently decrease the debt balance to get it in line with actual market values. The owner of the loan will receive the same total income and total loan payments, but a greater percentage of the income from debt service will be interest. Although he agrees to reduce the amount of the loan, he will receive the same total income.

The benefit of this technique is that the debt balance is lowered to a point closer to, and hopefully lower than, the market value, thereby increasing the potential for a sale. The total of monthly payments is about the same for a $22,000 note bearing 7% interest with payments of $150 per month, as for a note for $16,800 at 10% interest with payments of $150 a month. The number of payments, and consequently the amortization term, is virtually the same in both cases (about 28 years). The only differences are the lowering of the face amount of the note and an increase in the interest rate. To protect the holder of the note, you may want to prohibit its early payoff unless the holder gives written permission. With this type of debt renegotiation, you can place the property in a realistic marketing position and, in extreme problem cases, eliminate a suit when the property is on the verge of being abandoned.

NEGOTIATE LOWER PROPERTY TAXES

When you are acquiring distressed property, present the economics of the income to the tax appeals board, showing the true value of the property based on its economic performance. If you can get the taxes lowered until you improve the property's performance, it can work to everyone's benefit, even the taxing authority's. When you build the operation back up, chances are that the property taxes can be justifiably increased.

NEGOTIATE A MORATORIUM ON DEBT SERVICE

Distressed property can be a source of opportunity if you go into the acquisition with a solution-oriented plan. Often the first step is to develop a little breathing room by finding time to work out the difficulties causing the problem. Negotiating a freeze in the debt service payments could be the answer.

Lenders can be helpful in certain cases, especially when you throw the keys on the table. Really, they don't want the property back, and if you can demonstrate a well-thought-out and well-timed program to get the project back on sound footing, they will more than likely work with you.

ALWAYS TRY FOR RELEASE CLAUSES

If you are buying land, always try to negotiate for the release of an appropriate percentage of the total property as you reduce the loan principal. Releases often prove to be of special importance in determining the value of the property in the future. Furthermore, you can avoid the necessity of paying off the entire debt balance before getting construction financing if you plan a gradual development. If you are forced to default on the balance of the debt, you will have part of the property free and clear. Releases are, in effect, a way to lower your risk.

NO PERSONAL LIABILITY

Investment property that is worth buying should have obvious and sufficient value and should not require personal liability on your part. If the seller is carrying a purchase money mortgage, insist on a clause that limits his recourse on default to repossession of the property. Do the same with institutional financing. This is sometimes more difficult to negotiate because of the vague policies you have to work under, but it is well worth the try.

Including an exculpatory clause in your real estate loans may seem like a minor protective item, but these are uncertain times (as always) and you should be careful to take the prudent steps that will protect what you have.

Appendix

Guidelines for Evaluating Real Estate Investments

Investment analysis can be a simple, direct, and accurate process when you have your personal objectives clearly in mind. You analyze to clarify choice. The choice is usually between alternative investment opportunities. But in real estate we sometimes don't have an array of properties to choose from like stocks on the Big Board. Consequently, the choice is often limited to whether the property will meet your investment objectives.

The generally accepted method of analyzing all investments is to determine the annual rate of return (percentage) you can expect on the capital you plan to commit to the venture. Normally, the rate of return is expected to increase as risk increases. Consequently, when you compare alternative investments, you are faced with the challenge of deciding acceptable trade-offs between return, risk, and the general unknowns of the future.

There are two factors to keep in mind when analyzing an investment:

1. The total dollar income from all sources that you estimate will be generated by the investment, and
2. The percentage rate of return on the capital invested represented by the total income.

When you have a fairly satisfactory idea of these two figures (estimates though they are) you can determine whether the benefits warrant either investment in the property or continuation of the search.

Analyzing an investment is a process of comparing the dollars you get out with the dollars you put in. It's this relationship that produces your rate of return. This percentage return is compensation for putting your capital at risk, foregoing liquidity, and in some cases allowing others to use it for a limited period of time.

When you put money in savings at 6% interest, the bank lends it out at a higher rate for profit. The interest you receive is in a sense rent paid by the bank for use of your money. The rate of return in this example is 6% ($60 ÷ $1000 = 6%). There's no capital growth here, just rent for the use of your money.

If you put $1000 in the stock market you must analyze a different set of variables to determine your return on investment. Here you have a choice of stocks that pay dividends and hold the potential for appreciation or loss. Therefore, to accurately measure your rate of return you must consider the contribution of dividend payments (if any) and the appreciation of the stock (if any). If the dividend on a $1000 stock investment is $40 and the stock increases in value to $1,100 during one year, what is your pre-tax rate of return before commissions? ($40 dividend plus $100 increase in value = $140 ÷ $1000 = 14%). The rate of return here is appropriately higher in view of the risk you take.

Of course, taxes, selling expenses, and inflation reduce your actual purchasing power. Since after-tax returns vary with different individual tax brackets, the common practice of thinking in pre-tax rates is the only practical way of rapidly comparing investment alternatives, or so goes the argument. But it's really not that difficult to adjust your return for the taxes you pay or save. In fact, it's essential in a real estate investment because of the tax benefits. And it's not much more of a problem to plug in a factor for inflation and its reduction in the purchasing power of your invested capital. When you know the procedure you can make these calculations rapidly using the adjustments appropriate for your situation.

Your rate of return is a percentage expression of the dollar yield produced by your capital investment over a given time period. Calculations are made on an annual basis either to compare trends of years past or to project possible performance in future years. The basic concept is the same for determining the performance of money placed in a savings account, the stock market, or real estate. When you establish a rate of return, you state the relationship between three variables: your initial investment, the income it produces, and the time required to produce the income.

Complexity enters when variables unique to each investment are not separated and defined clearly in terms of their essential components: dollars invested, dollars received, and time. Accurate investment analysis is more a process of isolating these three factors and studying their relationship than anything else. Look at your analysis work as a process of simplification, of putting unique variables in clear perspective.

This process can get out of hand, though, and can result in serious errors when compounding and discounting are used to establish the time value of your cash flows. But you can discipline yourself to avoid falling into that trap by sticking to a couple of rules and not being seduced by the magic of calculators. Don't trust any calculation that involves a process you don't fully understand, not because it's inaccurate, but because it's rather useless to rely on calculations that don't make sense to you personally. Furthermore, don't accept assumptions that don't fit the reality of your particular investment. The reason for making assumptions when doing analysis work is to adjust the projections to the details of the project. A calculation process that forces unreal assumptions on you can result in a distorted and unreal rate of return. If you don't understand it, don't trust it. Any procedure that purports to be useful can be understood; if not, it probably is inaccurate.

When you consider the role of time in an investment you have an opportunity to improve significantly the return on the venture. If you reinvest the cash produced by your investment rather than spend it, you literally compound the benefits. By immediately reinvesting the cash flows of an investment, you generate a return on your return (interest on interest). In certain business ventures it is possible to reinvest the cash flows internally for expansion. The return under these circumstances is appropriately referred to as an internal rate of return. This concept is not unlike the internal compounding of annual dollar appreciation, characteristic of real estate in general, and land in particular. The dollar value of appreciation over time is not removed from the venture, but compounds internally until you refinance or sell.

Many investments, however, do produce cash flows each year, so if you want to trace accurately the future benefits of a venture, you must account for the effect of time on your initial investment and the cash flow it produces. For example, in forecasting the performance of a potential investment, you have the opportunity to increase the growth of your capital by immediately reinvesting the cash flows in a money market fund. The following comparison demonstrates how important solid money management is to your investment success.

Suppose you have $40,000 invested in rental property and you want to decide whether to spend or to save the cash flow. Although you have an idea of how it will feel to drive the new car you could buy, you want to evaluate the alternative of saving at 8% before it's too late.

Consumed By Spending	*End of Year 1*	*Year 2*	*Year 3*	*Year 4*	*Year 5*
Cash Flows (Net Rent)	$2,000	$3,000	$4,000	$ 5,000	$ 6,000
Rate of Return	5%	7.5%	10%	12.5%	15%
Accumulated Capital	0	0	0	0	0
Compounded By Savings					
Cash Flows (Net Rent)	$2,000	$3,000	$4,000	$ 5,000	$ 6,000
Cash Flows (Interest)	0	160	573	1,339	2,566
Total Cash Flows		3,160	4,573	6,339	8,566
Rate of Return	5%	7.9%	11.4%	15.8%	21.4%
Accumulated Capital	$2,000	$5,160	$9,573	$15,339	$22,566

If you want rapid capital growth, reinvest your investment income: don't spend it or at least not all of it. Note that the fifth-year return on the initial $40,000 investment is 6% greater when income is reinvested.

When you are evaluating the relative worth of investments, it's helpful to compare the benefits of a stagnant investment with an appreciating investment. In this example, assume that there is a $40,000 investment in free and clear land. One investor buys correctly and his property appreciates. The other investor buys at the wrong place at the wrong time and his investment stagnates. What is the effect of inflation and appreciation on these two ventures?

Stagnant Investment	*End of Year 1*	*Year 2*	*Year 3*	*Year 4*	*Year 5*
Rate of Appreciation	0%	0%	0%	0%	0%
Adjustment for 8% Inflation	−3,200	−2,944	−2,708	−2,492	−2,292
Value of Capital Invested	$36,800	$33,856	$31,148	$28,656	$26,364
Appreciating Investment					
Rate of Appreciation	9%	11%	15%	20%	25%
Adjustment for 8% Inflation (Net)	+400	+1,212	+2,913	+5,343	+8,478
Value of Capital Invested	$40,400	$41,612	$44,525	$49,868	$58,345

If you don't have any cash flow in a non-appreciating investment, you'll eventually lose your purchasing power in an inflationary economy. But, if you invest wisely you receive the compounding benefits of appreciation which offset the purchasing power lost to inflation.

There's really no easy, safe alternative to paying careful attention to your investment capital. If it's sitting in a losing portfolio, it's just a matter of time before you have little or nothing left. Capital growth is essential to survival in today's economy.

How you manage your money effects your return as much as the type of investment you choose. For the same $40,000 capital outlay you can have a choice of investment benefits, each of which contributes to your return. The important decision-making objective of investment analysis is to determine which investment is most profitable. Isolating the rate of return is essential if you want to compare different investments. But if you only look at the return on cash flow, you may miss other significant contributors to your investment growth. No doubt any financial benefit can be stated as a cash flow and measured in relation to time. But for our purposes now, it is sufficient to spotlight the effect of individual benefits on your rate of return. When you isolate the return-generating benefits of an investment and single out the percentage contribution of each to your capital growth, you're on the way to understanding the truly outstanding characteristics of real estate. Following this chain of logic to its natural conclusion, let's look at the combined benefits of a real estate investment illustrated in the following chart. Notice that the appreciation rate is applied to the total value of the property ($200,000) not just the capital invested ($40,000 down payment). This is an illustration of the power of leverage. Also, leverage is at the root of the contribution to growth of equity build-up. Each year the amount of loan reduction adds to your investment growth.

The purpose of the following form is to demonstrate that the benefits of any investment can be evaluated in terms of their individual contributions to the venture. Certainly you can go further in your analysis if you like. Discounted cash flow analysis and computer modeling hold great promise. In fact, there's no end to the approaches available for analyzing real estate. But they are only useful to the extent that they provide a more accurate and easily understood basis for evaluating your risk and return. Eventually, no matter which mathematical approach you take, in the end you must rely on your common sense judgment to translate the numerical abstractions into cold hard dollars. It's that necessary and sufficient mathematical data that can give you the confidence to take action.

ANALYSIS OF RETURN ON INVESTMENT

Property Rawhide Apartments

INVESTMENT (including closing costs of $ 1000)* $ 40,000

I. CASH FLOW

Estimated Annual Gross Spendable Income $ 2000

or Cash Return on Investment of . . . . 5 %

II. EQUITY BUILDUP

Annual loan payments of $ 17,110 less Interest

of $ 15,600 amounts to Equity Buildup of $ 1510

which is equal to a return of . . . . 3.8 %

III. TAX SAVINGS

Ist year tax loss of $ 5421 in the 35 % tax

bracket results in estimated tax savings of $ 1897

or return on investment of . . . . 4.7 %

IV. APPRECIATION

Property values in this vicinity have appreciated at

the rate of approximately 5 % per year recently.

This would result in an increase in value of $ 10,000

or an additional return on investment of. . . . . 25 %

V. TOTAL NET RETURN ON INVESTMENT

I plus II plus III plus IV. . . . . $ 15,407 38.5 %

* Closing Costs: Estimated costs of transaction. Some of these costs may be depreciation items, added to the basis of property for tax purposes.

Index

R

S

T

U

V

W